HOBBS OF HENLEY

A History

Simon Wenham

AMBERLEY

Front cover (top): a postcard from 1919 showing the Hobbs and Sons rental site off New Street. (Author's collection)

Front cover (bottom): *Hibernia* passing through Henley Bridge. (© Sue Milton of www. thames-cards.co.uk)

First published 2020

Amberley Publishing
The Hill, Stroud
Gloucestershire, GL5 4EP

www.amberleybooks.com

Copyright © Simon Wenham, 2020

The right of Simon Wenham to be identified as the Author
of this work has been asserted in accordance with the
Copyrights, Designs and Patents Act 1988.

British Library Cataloguing in Publication Data.
A catalogue record for this book is available from the British Library.

ISBN 978 1 4456 9660 7 (print)
ISBN 978 1 4456 9661 4 (ebook)

Typesetting by Aura Technology and Software Services, India.
Printed in Great Britain.

Contents

Introduction

Low in a vale, by wood-crown'd heights 'erhung;
Where larch and fir, and beech are careless flung;
With silver Thames slow rolling at her feet;
Lies Henley – contemplation's calm retreat.

'Henley: a Poem', *c.* 1827[1]

The Thames flows through many historic locations, but the place that perhaps epitomises recreation on the river more than any other is Henley-on-Thames, the home of Britain's most famous regatta. Its evocative name conjures up idealised images of balmy weather, boats, blazers, picnics, pavilions and parties. The quintessential rowing town not only hosts one of the most colourful and celebrated events of the social calendar, but it also draws in large numbers of tourists each year. Most of those who want to experience the charms of the Thames from the water turn to the services of Hobbs of Henley.

This book, written to mark the firm's 150th anniversary, is the first to tell in detail the story of the historic river business that became a notable boatbuilder, rental provider and passenger boat operator, as well as an important local employer with bases in a number of nearby locations. Furthermore, in the past century, the family has produced four mayors of the town, a Member of the British Empire, and two Watermen to the Queen.[2]

Background: The Hobbs of Hambleden

The Hobbs family has lived in the Hambleden area (near Henley) for centuries. One genealogical study traced their lineage back to a Thomas Hobbs, born in 1490. By the seventeenth century many of his descendants were farmers in the Hambleden valley, while others had spread to nearby Medmenham and Great Marlow. A key development was in 1621, when two of them, Thomas Hobbs, and his son, William, started to rent the sizeable Burrow Farm from Balliol College. Indeed, the family, who would have sublet parts of the estate, were in situ during the English Civil War, when soldiers regularly passed through the area and nearby riverside properties, like Greenlands, were fortified. The date is highly significant for another reason, as it shows that the family's association with the river is far earlier than they realised, because the property, which they retained until 1808, included the wharf next to (and downstream of) Hambleden Mill. The waterways were thriving arteries of trade at the time and the agricultural area was well known for its timber, malt and corn, much of which was transported by barge. The flour mill, which was one of the last to survive on the Thames, supplied the Huntley and Palmer biscuit factory in Reading until the 1950s, before being converted into luxury flats in the early 1980s.

The family was important by the eighteenth century. In 1709, William Hobbs was the Constable of Hambleden, whose duties included collecting rates, inspecting alehouses, training the local militia, convening parish meetings, suppressing gaming houses and riots, detaining criminals, collecting child maintenance from fathers of illegitimate children, supervising strangers and beggars, and arresting escaped prisoners. His son, of the same name, became a tythingman, responsible for enforcing some of the law relating to the division of farming units. By 1775, Thomas (great-great-grandfather of Harry, who started the Henley business) and his brother, Francis, were both Deputies for Hambleden (with the latter also becoming a tythingman).[3]

The *Posse Comitatus*, a survey commissioned in 1798 to count the able-bodied men aged between fifteen and sixty years of age who might be called upon in the event of an invasion by Napoleon, illustrates how difficult it is to discern who was related to whom at that time. Fifteen Hobbs are listed in the small parish of Hambleden, six of whom were called John and four of whom were named William. Their occupations are shown as labourers (four individuals), wharfingers (three), an apprentice, servant, victualler, cordwainer, dealer, tailor, baker and an owner of eight horses, three wagons and two carts. Rather confusingly the wharfingers (owners of a wharf) are recorded as John Hobbs, John Hobbs senior, John Hobbs junior and William Plummer.

The earliest written record of the family working on the river is the death certificate of Margaret Hobbs in 1756, which listed her husband, Thomas, as a wharfinger. A further three generations continued in the role, including their son and grandson, who were presumably the Johns (senior and junior) mentioned in the *Posse Comitatus*. The last wharfinger appears to have been the latter's son, Henry, who was still in the profession at Mill End Wharf in 1861. Indeed, Fred Thacker's survey of the locks and weirs of the river records that there was a Henry operating the nearby Aston Ferry in 1854 (for a wage of 18s per month, reduced from 24s), who then resigned his post in 1870, as well as a Thomas Hobbs listed there by the Thames Conservancy in 1866. Incidentally, the publican at the nearby Flower Pot inn, which the Aston Ferry served, was James Arlett, whose descendants went on to establish a rival boating business in Henley. When Henry passed away in 1890, his obituary in the *Bucks Herald* claimed there had been Hobbs working on the river well before 1756. It reported that he came from 'one of the oldest families in the parish, as he and his ancestors had held the Wharf for over 200 years'. Furthermore, he had been the long-standing collector of the Queen's taxes and was said to be an honest and good man, who had the 'rare faculty of minding his own business'. Today, the Mill End wharf cottage is a Grade II listed building and although it has a brick on it marked with 'J. H. 1755' (John Hobbs), part of it is believed to date back to the seventeenth century.

When it came to the family's involvement in Henley, it was a tale of two other Henry Hobbs, who were both descendants of William Hobbs (b. 1674), the father of Thomas, the wharfinger. One was the son of John, who was running the Angel pub by 1838, which was the primary 'rowing-house' of the town, as well as the main location for hiring punts for fishing and pleasure boats. Their association with the Thames was cut short in tragic circumstances. In March 1840, Henry and two friends took advantage of some windy weather to go sailing, only for a squall to tip the boat over and cause it to sink rapidly. The others managed to get to the bank, but Henry, who was described as a 'young man respected for his quiet and obliging manners', was not so fortunate. The trauma led to his father putting up the inn for sale, partly because Henry, his only son, had been in charge of the boating side of the business. It was not until 1843, however, that the family found a buyer and moved to the George and Dragon at Marlow.

An eerie postscript to the story is that in 1845, only five years after the sailing incident, the successor at the Angel, Henry Rogerson, also drowned in windy conditions. He and his nephew died after falling into fast-flowing water, when the towing rope they were using to bring back a sculling boat from Windsor caused the craft to tip over.

It was a year after the drowning of Henry Hobbs that his relative and namesake (known as Harry) was born. He was the second son of John, a labourer (and later carpenter), and Harriet Hobbs (née Lawrence), a laundress, who lived together on the north side of Henley on the Marlow Road. Although the oldest son, John (b. 1838), became a tailor and moved from Henley, both Harry (carpenter) and his younger sister, Mary (laundress), adopted the

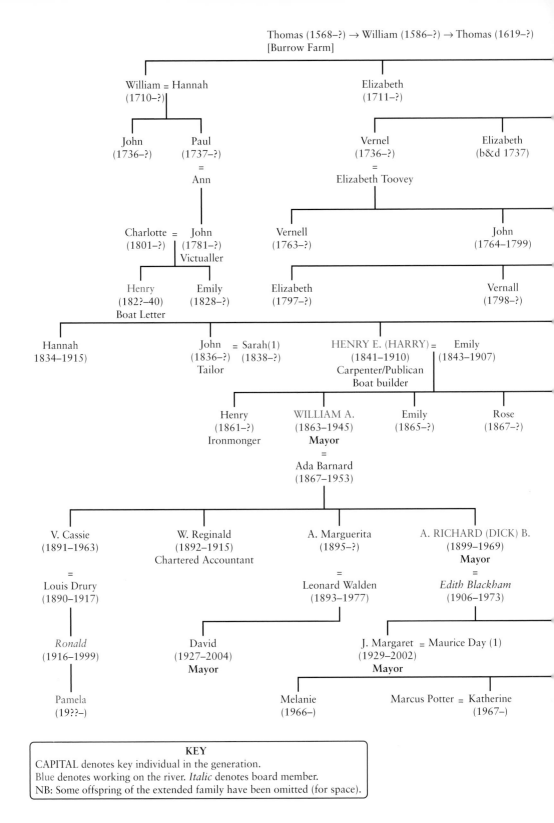

Thomas (1568–?) → William (1586–?) → Thomas (1619–?)
[Burrow Farm]

William = Hannah
(1710–?)

Elizabeth
(1711–?)

John
(1736–?)

Paul
(1737–?)
=
Ann

Vernel
(1736–?)
=
Elizabeth Toovey

Elizabeth
(b&d 1737)

Charlotte =
(1801–?)

John
(1781–?)
Victualler

Vernell
(1763–?)

John
(1764–1799)

Henry
(182?–40)
Boat Letter

Emily
(1828–?)

Elizabeth
(1797–?)

Vernall
(1798–?)

Hannah
1834–1915)

John
(1836–?)
Tailor

= Sarah(1)
(1838–?)

HENRY E. (HARRY) =
(1841–1910)
Carpenter/Publican
Boat builder

Emily
(1843–1907)

Henry
(1861–?)
Ironmonger

WILLIAM A.
(1863–1945)
Mayor
=
Ada Barnard
(1867–1953)

Emily
(1865–?)

Rose
(1867–?)

V. Cassie
(1891–1963)
=
Louis Drury
(1890–1917)

W. Reginald
(1892–1915)
Chartered Accountant

A. Marguerita
(1895–?)
=
Leonard Walden
(1893–1977)

A. RICHARD (DICK) B.
(1899–1969)
Mayor
=
Edith Blackham
(1906–1973)

Ronald
(1916–1999)

David
(1927–2004)
Mayor

J. Margaret = Maurice Day (1)
(1929–2002)
Mayor

Pamela
(19??–)

Melanie
(1966–)

Marcus Potter = Katherine
(1967–)

KEY
CAPITAL denotes key individual in the generation.
Blue denotes working on the river. *Italic* denotes board member.
NB: Some offspring of the extended family have been omitted (for space).

6

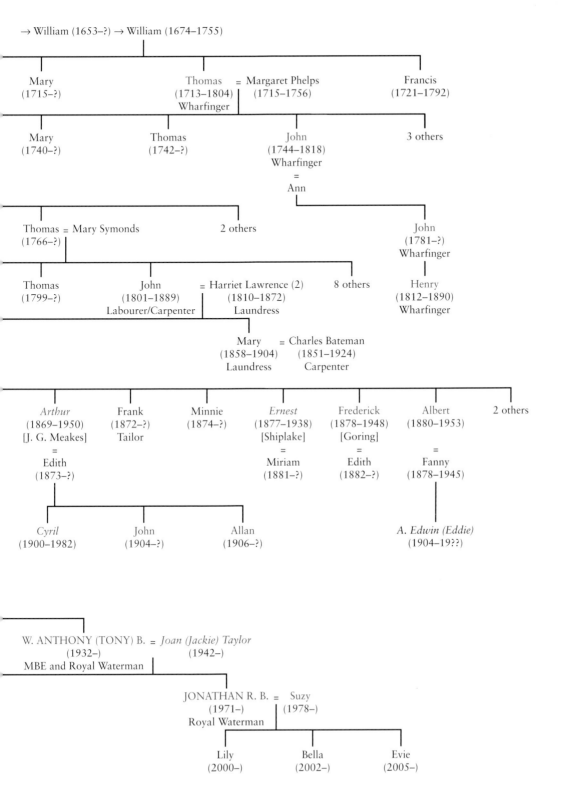

→ William (1653–?) → William (1674–1755)

Mary (1715–?) · Thomas (1713–1804) Wharfinger = Margaret Phelps (1715–1756) · Francis (1721–1792)

Mary (1740–?) · Thomas (1742–?) · John (1744–1818) Wharfinger = Ann · 3 others

Thomas (1766–?) = Mary Symonds · 2 others · John (1781–?) Wharfinger

Thomas (1799–?) · John (1801–1889) Labourer/Carpenter = Harriet Lawrence (2) (1810–1872) Laundress · 8 others · Henry (1812–1890) Wharfinger

Mary (1858–1904) Laundress = Charles Bateman (1851–1924) Carpenter

Arthur (1869–1950) [J. G. Meakes] = Edith (1873–?) · Frank (1872–?) Tailor · Minnie (1874–?) · Ernest (1877–1938) [Shiplake] = Miriam (1881–?) · Frederick (1878–1948) [Goring] = Edith (1882–?) · Albert (1880–1953) = Fanny (1878–1945) · 2 others

Cyril (1900–1982) · John (1904–?) · Allan (1906–?) · A. Edwin (Eddie) (1904–19??)

W. ANTHONY (TONY) B. (1932–) MBE and Royal Waterman = Joan (Jackie) Taylor (1942–)

JONATHAN R. B. (1971–) Royal Waterman = Suzy (1978–)

Lily (2000–) · Bella (2002–) · Evie (2005–)

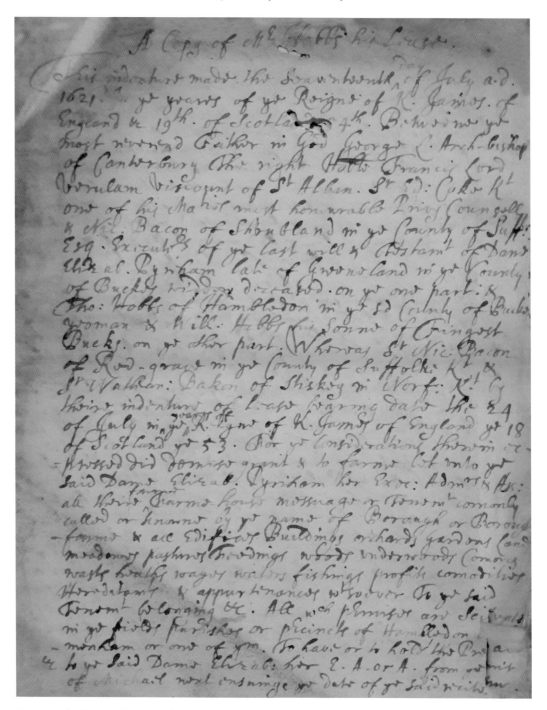

Contract for Burrow Farm, 1621
The contract for Burrow Farm between Balliol College (owner) and Thomas and William
Hobbs (tenants), dated 1621. (© Reproduced by kind permission of the Master and Fellows of
Balliol College)

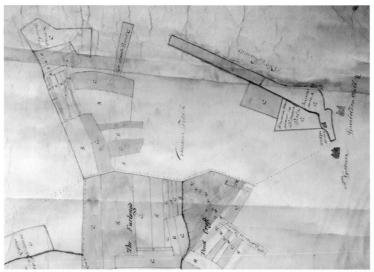

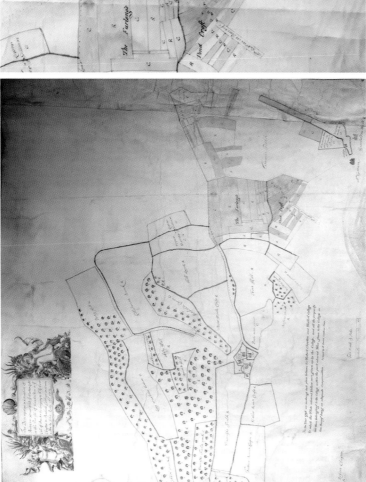

Burrow Farm Map, 1701
A map of Burrow Farm from 1701 (largely matching an earlier, but less clear map from 1616). The image on the right is an enlarged version of the bottom right section of the bigger map and it shows the Thames running alongside the thin strip of land with Hambleden Mill next to it (the building in the bottom right corner). (© Reproduced by kind permission of the Master and Fellows of Balliol College)

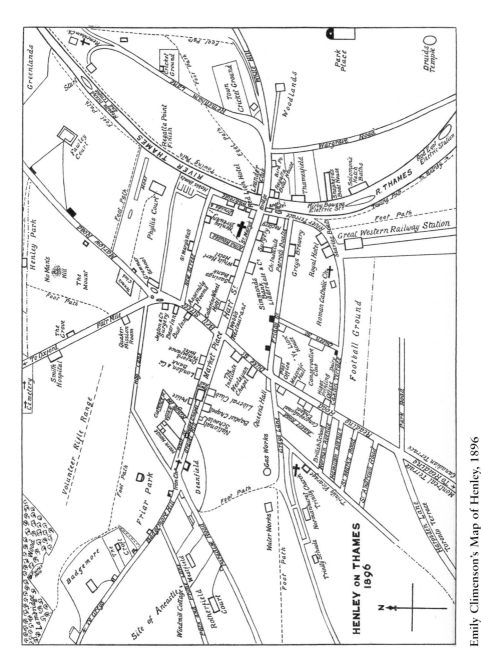

Emily Climenson's Map of Henley, 1896

Emily Climenson's map of Henley from her guidebook of 1896 that shows the main boat companies, the swimming baths and many of the town sites connected with the Hobbs family.

Right: **Harry Hobbs**
Harry Hobbs (1841–1910), the founder of the Henley business and the publican of the Ship from 1871. (© Hobbs of Henley)

Below: **Old Ship House**
Old Ship House on Wharfe Lane, a private home that was once the Ship, a diminutive pub (the section to the right) that had guest quarters (the section to the left). (© Simon Wenham)

trades of their parents. The latter married Charles Bateman, another carpenter, who in 1924 would drown near Hobbs' yard after going for a walk.

Harry married Emily and, in 1861, they had the first of their twelve children, Henry, who went on to become an ironmonger. In April 1871, Harry became the licensee of the Ship, a diminutive waterside pub off New Street (now Wharfe Lane) dating back to the 1760s. The Hobbs took over the premises from the Hoopers, a boatbuilding family from Oxford. The relocation was only a short distance, but it had long-term ramifications, as it brought them into direct contact with a whole new aquatic world. The pub was situated by what had been the town's most substantial wharf of the seventeenth century and it was also one of a number of drinking establishments in Henley that rented out pleasure boats.

Yet while Harry was forging his new career in the 1880s, his father would spend his final years in the almshouse by St Mary's Church, where his older sister, Hannah, would also end up in 1903; in her case, after a lucky thirteenth attempt to be admitted by ballot. In an interesting twist of fate, this was the establishment that their descendants would subsequently help to run (see chapter 6).[4]

Dating the Business

The firm uses the slogan 'The best in boating since 1870', but it is not entirely clear when the business began, because Harry did not take over the Ship until the following year. It is quite possible, therefore, that the family simply got it wrong, though that seems unlikely, because the earlier date was quoted in an advertisement written at the turn of the century, when the founder was still alive. So Harry may have had some connection with the river or the pub prior to becoming the licensee of the Ship, but unfortunately there is no record it. The issue is further complicated by Hobbs advertising in the mid-1930s (in the official *Guide to Henley*) that it was established in 1892. It was around that time that the firm started to refer more regularly in its marketing to when it was founded, although by the late 1950s the date had been revised back to 1870.

Although the mystery may never be resolved, it is clear that the family's association with the river extends a lot further back, to 1621 and their involvement with Burrow Farm and the wharf in Mill End. That was well before the Henley brewers Brakspears were even in the drinks industry. Coincidentally, it also means that 2021 is a year of anniversaries: the family's 400th on the river and the firm's 150th since Harry took over the pub.[5]

Henley in the Victorian Period

By 1871, Henley, which was often wrongly described in guidebooks at the time as the oldest town in Oxfordshire, was still relatively small in size with only four main roads and 3,735 inhabitants (or 5,034 including Rotherfield Greys). It still retained much of its rural charm with red squirrels in the trees and hundreds of hares populating the fields, flanking its southern border (where the St Mark's estate now is). The town was an important crossing place of the river, however – with a toll being collected on the bridge until 1873 – and a lot of traffic inevitably passed through it.

The family's relocation to the Ship could hardly have been better timed, as Henley was rapidly developing into a highly fashionable and bustling resort, owing to its enviable scenery, proximity to London and the burgeoning reputation of its annual regatta (first held in 1839). It was the opening of the railway station in 1857, a development encouraged by the leading townsfolk, which was key in drawing in large numbers of visitors from the surrounding area and the capital in particular. As Abel Heywood's 1882 guidebook put it,

Henley was 'one of the most agreeable spots to visit, for boating men, anglers, pedestrians, and lovers of quiet rural scenes and pleasures', and was 'not only one of the prettiest towns on the river, but also one of the healthiest'. By the mid-1890s, there were twenty-eight trains arriving in the town per day in the winter and far more during the summer.[6] This was during a period that has been described as the 'golden age of the Thames' (*c.* 1880–1914), when vast numbers of people flocked to the waterway to take part in the craze for pleasure boating. Indeed, the river above London was transformed from a working waterway into a vast conduit of pleasure, characterised by boat outings, steam launch trips, Venetian fairs, regattas, picnics and carnivals.

The railway played another part in this overall transformation by destroying much of the commercial barge trade, which not only starved the river authorities of income and led to a new stronger organisation (the Thames Conservancy) being formed, but also freed up a lot of waterside property to be reinvented for other uses. Many entrepreneurial individuals tried to capitalise on the booming pleasure boat market, but ultimately few enjoyed long-term success. Indeed, this book, which focuses on the social side of the business rather than its financial performance, explores how Hobbs managed to succeed where so many others failed. It also examines how, in the process, it became one of the best-known and longest-standing businesses in Henley and on the river.

Chapter 1

Pleasure Boating

Hobbs used to boast of having more boats than the Royal Navy. They probably still do – but it's no longer such a proud boast.

John Eade[1]

Waterside taverns played an important role in popularising pleasure boating. In 1866, one guidebook to the river recorded that the Ship was one of only three Henley pubs that rented out craft. The received wisdom from the family was that, initially, Harry Hobbs probably only had a small number of vessels (probably punts) at his disposal to hire out to anglers. That rings true with how boating developed in other locations, such as the upper tidal Thames, where many watermen rented craft out for fishing as sidelines, only to then focus more heavily on the market as it became increasingly popular.

Henley was known for being 'one of the most favourite places of pilgrimage for anglers'[2] and Abel Heywood's guidebook (1882) reported that a notable feature of the waterfront was the 'Punts moored by poles mid-stream, where men sit in rush-bottom chairs'. Angling could be done without charge, but Emily Climenson reported in 1896 that professional fishermen – of whom there were seven in total by the end of the century, including those from other river families, like William Parrott (junior and senior) and George Arlett – could be hired to assist one's efforts. Trout, pike, perch, roach, dace, carp, chub, barbell, tench, gudgeon, bleak, bream, eels, minnows, popes and ruffs were all said to be readily available. Indeed, the leading authority on all things piscatorial – not to mention meteorological, as the official recorder of rainfall – was none other than A. Edward Hobbs (no immediate relation), a prominent architect and town councillor who posthumously had a Henley pub named after him. He was one of the most famous Thames anglers of the era who caught hundreds of trout in his lifetime, some of which are mounted in the River and Rowing Museum. He also wrote extensively about the angling scene, as Honorary Secretary of the Henley Fishing Preservation Society.

Boating in the town was not all purely recreational at that time, however, as there was still some trade carried by water, even though much of it had ceased with the arrival of the railway. The Ship was located by (Robert) Webb's Wharf, which was named after the timber merchant and barge builder who was still running weekly barges to and from London into the 1880s. By 1896, Emily Climenson noted that these picturesque craft were 'rapidly disappearing' and were being 'transmogrified into ugly grimy steam tugs'. Furthermore, as there were not any other major bridges nearby, there were also a number of working ferries close by, such as at Wargrave, Mill End, and Medmenham.[3]

The 'Golden Age of the Thames'

The Ship probably did not have many boats by the early 1880s and it did not even get a mention in some of the Thames guides. Nevertheless, it would certainly have benefitted from the growing popularity of aquatic leisure, as between 1879 and 1887 lock toll receipts for small pleasure boats on the river above Staines more than doubled from £1,647 per annum to £3,805 per annum respectively.[4] Indeed, Abel Heywood's guidebook of 1882 described how the Thames was drawing people to the town:

> BOATING is one of the great attractions of Henley. Mention Henley to hundreds of city men, and it is not the Regatta of which they instantly conjure up pleasant pictures, but of quiet days on the river at Henley, or of camping out on its pleasant banks. Boats of all sizes may be had by the journey, the day, or the season, from the several boat proprietors.

As that suggests, although the population of Henley and Rotherfield Greys was rising sharply at the time (from 5,043 in 1881 to 6,130 by 1901), the area was much less busy than the hugely popular resorts closer to London. Molesey Lock (by Hampton Court Palace) was the 'headquarters' of a summer-long 'carnival on the river', while Boulter's Lock (Maidenhead) was the 'Piccadilly Circus' further upstream, especially on Ascot Sunday, held the weekend after the races, when spectators traditionally took to the water.[5]

During this 'golden age of the Thames' thousands of people dressed in boating attire could be seen congregating at stations in west London every weekend in the summer, waiting to go out to a resort for a 'Thames trip'. A good proportion of them were women, at a time when they were excluded from many recreational pastimes. Indeed, such mixing of the sexes was part of the appeal of the river for some, although it was also inevitably a concern for others.

Although the term 'golden age' conjures up a wholly positive image, the Thames was so popular by the 1880s that there were considerable tensions between different waterway users. The painter G. D. Leslie of Goring, who was fond of punting, was one who complained bitterly about the arrival of 'beanfeasters out for a trip on the river' (people on a company outing), as well as 'country bumpkins' who were 'nearly as bad'. While steamboats were often derided by those on manually powered craft, one activity that was a particular nuisance for landowners because of the damage caused was camping. This pastime was first popularised as a leisure activity on the Thames, as boats were ideal for carrying the heavy equipment and a number of rental operators even produced vessels that converted into floating tents. The reported crimes of those taking part in this emerging activity included boiling kettles with fire made from the landowner's cherished pea-sticks, injuring horses with broken glass from champagne bottles, littering with newspapers, climbing garden walls, stealing fruit and eggs, and surreptitiously milking cows at 'unholy hours'. While things do not seem to have got out of hand in Henley, where the principle camping sites were the bathing place off Wargrave Road and Regatta Island, the situation was far worse closer to London. Riverside tenants near Bisham Abbey, for example, were even demanding lower rent because of all the parties trying to use their property.

The many tensions eventually led to the passing of the 1885 Thames Preservation Act that sought to protect the river that had become 'largely used as a place of public recreation and resort', by defining more clearly the rights of boaters and riparian landowners. By that stage some were already avoiding the waterway. In 1886, the *Pall Mall Gazette* declared that the Thames was no longer a place for a holiday, because of ''Arry [working-class Londoners] camping in rows of tents on the lock islands, house-boats anchored against every available bank, [and] launches destructive of peace and property rushing up and down.' Worst of all was the realisation that most respectable people considered those on the water to be pests.[6]

Although Henley may not have been overrun by campers, Emily Climenson's guide gives a flavour of just how busy the river had become by the end of the nineteenth century. She recorded that there were *twelve* boat companies operating in the small town (see chapter 4), while many could still remember when the total number of pleasure boats could be counted on the fingers of your hands. Despite the competition, Hobbs expanded from the end of the nineteenth century onwards (see chapter 5) and, by the interwar period, it was not only offering a large range of small craft for hire, such as punts, canoes and rowing craft, but also steam and electric launches.

Although pleasure boating on the river then suffered from the Thames Conservancy increasing the lock tolls after the First World War, Henley remained, as the *Evening News* put it, 'a superb playground for the metropolitan millions'. The 'modern Elysium', which it claimed was renowned for the attractive girls who visited it, boasted reasonably priced accommodation and a river that belonged to the people with glorious walks on both of its banks.[7]

In 1925, Hobbs claimed to have 'a stock of 120 Punts and an equal number of Dinghies, Canoes and Boats, for Hire by the Hour, Day or Season'. The firm would also have had more craft outside of Henley, such as the motor launch *Nectar* and seventy-five 'punts, boats, dinghies and canoes' it acquired in 1940, when it bought Ashley's yard in Pangbourne (see chapter 5).

Webb's Wharf
A painting of Webb's Wharf (1889) attributed to Janet Cooper. Robert Webb was a timber merchant and barge builder whose firm operated a weekly barge to London into the 1880s.
(© River and Rowing Museum, Henley-on-Thames)

HOBBS & SONS, LTD.,
HENLEY-ON-THAMES.

BUILDERS
and
DESIGNERS
of
STEAM
and
ELECTRIC
LAUNCHES.

"MARGHERITA," ELECTRIC LAUNCH.
Length 45ft.   Beam 6ft.
(FOR HIRE).

Margherita
The 45-foot *Margherita*, an electric launch the firm rented out in the late 1890s. (© Hobbs of Henley)

The punt was the favoured craft in the early twentieth century and it was also a vessel that was particularly suited to the inevitable 'crush' of boats at busy events. Not only was it sturdy, but it could easily raft against other craft, as it lacked the oars and outriggers that could catch on other vessels. Although the town hosted a number of regular rowing events, the boating season was dominated by one event that outshone all others: the Henley Royal Regatta.

The Henley Royal Regatta

It was the natural landscape of Henley that enabled the town to develop into one of the leading rowing centres of the country. The universities of Oxford and Cambridge took advantage of the long, straight and relatively wide section of the Thames to hold the first boat race against each other in 1829. The event inspired the townsfolk to hold an annual regatta from 1839 onwards. It attracted huge crowds and its reputation was bolstered further by receiving royal patronage from Prince Albert in 1851. As one commentator in the *Evening News* put it, there was 'no brighter or more joyous place on earth than Henley-on-Thames in Regatta week'.

In 1891, the *Lock to Lock Times* described some of the familiar faces that you saw during the festivities, including the letter of lodgings (whose income ensured he was 'an easy winner'), the 'bluff and hearty' houseboat host (with 'as many difference shades of character as you can think of'), the hopeful and anxious competitor, the distinguished actor and popular actress, the 'negro minstrel', the loving young picnickers (who were

17

uninterested in the rowing), the gipsy fortune-teller (pouncing on stray lunching parties), the first-class ticket (who ends up in third class), the third-class ticket (who is happy to slip into first class), and the all-important course clearer. The latter had to keep the vast flotilla from massing into the path of the races, which is why the author claimed he would be underpaid, if he was on less than £2,000 for the three days. Indeed, over 35,000 people arrived by GWR train alone for the three days of events at the end of the century (around 10,000 more than were arriving on the eve of the First World War). This inevitably put a strain on the infrastructure of the town and, in 1902, one pumping station had to deal with over 200,000 gallons of sewage in twenty-four hours (the equivalent of 35 gallons per head of the normal population!).

The Hobbs boathouses (by the Ship) enjoyed an enviable position, as they were located near the finish line of the original course and were therefore often referred to in reports of the races as notable landmarks. Indeed, the pub was well patronised, as is shown by Harry Hobbs applying to be able to serve alcohol from 4 a.m. during the contest in 1885. The move was in stark contrast to a century later, when magistrates were trying to reduce the drinking hours during the event. As Neil Wigglesworth points out, after the firm acquired a further site south of the bridge on Station Road (1898), many visitors 'would have strolled the few paces from the station around the corner to Hobbs' boatyard to hire some form of craft in which to disport themselves to the utter dismay of the regatta officials'.

Given the number of spectators, it is unsurprising that prices 'ruled high' during the showpiece event. If the weather was nice, boat-letters were often sold out of craft by lunchtime, even though many extra vessels were brought to the town by other businesses (and by Hobbs from its other yards). One can get an idea of the price inflation from the storage fees for craft in 1909, which during the regatta rose fourfold from 2s 6d (the normal rate for a week) to 10s. The charge for renting out a small vessel at the event was around 25s.

Unlike some other firms, Hobbs did not hire out houseboats, although their launch *Marian* was among the many craft that moored along the course during the Edwardian period. Indeed, in 1896, Emily Climenson recorded that the Thames Conservancy was driven wild in the run-up to the event, having to assign places for over eighty houseboats and other craft that stretched all the way from the bridge to beyond Temple Island. Although the rowing event's popularity fluctuated over time, it remained the most important annual fixture in the calendar for Hobbs.[8]

World Wars

In both world wars, the major rowing contests were all cancelled, but the firm continued to rent out craft. Although there was a heightened fear of German spies in Henley during the First World War, the town was relatively quiet with most guest houses lying empty. One notable sight on the Thames was the Royal Engineers practising building pontoons across the river and then galloping horses across them. When the Armistice was finally declared in 1918, the news was greeted by a cacophony of sirens, motor horns, detonators and church bells. The employees of Stuart Turner, who had recently built Ernest Shackleton's electrical lighting plant for his ship *Endurance*, spilled out onto the street to join the many citizens 'wreathed in smiles', as well as shedding tears for the lost.

During the Second World War, Henley's air-raid siren went off 260 times, but, again, the town remained relatively unscathed, although its population was transformed by the arrival of many evacuees. While commercial barge traffic rose significantly on the river, pleasure boating initially declined, before becoming hugely popular in the latter stages of the conflict. The change was partly the result of southern seaside resorts being closed off, as well as the

'Holidays at Home' movement. Although the motorboats were rendered immobile by the fuel restrictions and the rental canoes were commandeered by the Royal Marines for the training of swimmer canoeists, the camping craft were once again highly popular. Indeed, Tony Hobbs' first job was assisting his father in nearby Shiplake, which involved keeping the tent boats stocked up with all the necessary equipment, including filling up the Primus stoves.

One of his most vivid memories was witnessing the US Air Force B-17 Flying Fortress bomber *Sunrise Serenader* crashing near Wargrave on 13 November 1943. There were many American servicemen in the local area – and one of them, Private John Waters, became infamous for murdering his evacuee girlfriend, Doris Staples, in Henley that same year – but this particular crew had flown from Northamptonshire. The aeroplane was struck by lightning when passing through a thunderhead, which ripped a hole in some of the bodywork and started a fire on board. The pilot managed to regain control and, after flying low over Henley and turning away from a collision course with Wargrave, attempted to crash land. The crew jettisoned the eight 500-lb bombs and one of them, Alan Purdy, parachuted out shortly before the plane exploded and descended in a fireball. Tony and his father jumped into punts and went across the river to see if they could provide assistance, but

The crew of *Sunrise Serenader*
The crew of *Sunrise Serenader*, a B-17 Flying Fortress that Tony Hobbs witnessed crashing near Wargrave on 13 November 1943. This photograph was taken in South Dakota in the summer of 1943 and shows nine of the ten men who were on board, including the sole survivor, Alan Purdy (furthest right). (© Wargrave Local History Society)

Postcard, 1904
A postcard from 1904 showing 'the crush' of boats during the regatta. (Author's collection)

it was obvious that nothing could be done for the remaining nine crew members on board. A group of those who witnessed the crash subsequently contacted relatives of the airmen and a memorial service was held for them on 13 November 2014, attended by Theresa May, the local MP (and future Prime Minister).

When the war eventually ended, once again Stuart Turner's employees played a prominent part in the proceedings. Some of them paraded through the town as pallbearers carrying a coffin that contained an effigy of Hitler, which was dumped onto a large bonfire.[9]

The 'Second Golden Age of the Thames'

In the third quarter of the twentieth century there was a notable rise in pleasure boating. Between 1956 and 1973, the number of registered vessels on the river more than doubled, while the number passing through the locks more than tripled (to over a million craft), causing the Conservancy to abolish lock tolls in 1967. The years from 1973 to 1981 could be described as a 'second golden age of the Thames', as there were unprecedented numbers of craft travelling on the waterway, as the oil crisis and recession kept many people holidaying in the UK.

The river looked very different from the late nineteenth century, however, as the proliferation of fibreglass boats ended much of the traditional wooden boatbuilding on the river. Canoes were one casualty from rental fleets at the time, as they were less easy to build from the new material and were not sufficiently tough. Although the firm still had ninety manually powered craft by 1970 (canoes, punts, dinghies and skiffs), non-motorised craft were falling out of favour, including the once popular punts and camping craft. Although the last few of the latter remained at Goring, customers were preferring the more comfortable cabin cruisers. Indeed, the motorboat reigned supreme by the 1970s.

The busiest section of the river was between Henley and Boulter's Lock, where Simon Townley describes there being 'long lock queues on summer weekends, occasional conflict between anglers and motor launches, and regular use not only by rowers, but by canoeists and sailing boats'. In 1973, for example, Marsh Lock (by Henley) had more vessels passing through it (44,483) than any other on the river (a 12 per cent increase on the previous year).

As had been the case a century earlier, some river users claimed that the waterway was too overrun. As J. H. B. Peel put it, 'Britons so far as ruling the waves, are defeated by a tideless backwater.' In 1978, the Thames Water Authority made a number of recommendations to tackle the problem, which included preventing the creation of new river facilities. Tony Hobbs disagreed with the pronouncements, arguing that it was during the six-week school holiday that the river was very busy and, even then, it was only on the weekends that getting through locks was particularly slow. He criticised the water authority for becoming 'more and more bureaucratic', although he welcomed their suggestion of forming a Thames users' group.

There were similar discussions about the future of Henley too, as tourism was one of the fastest-growing markets and the town was attracting increasing numbers of visitors. There were differences of opinion about how to manage the influx, as well as whether or not to encourage even more people, but one innovation that was agreed upon was the creation of a tourist information point in the Town Hall (opened in 1983).

The waterway's popularity subsequently dropped, as economic recovery, the onset of cheap package holidays, and the rising cost of boating meant that fewer people vacationed on the river. In 2003, Eileen McKeever, Thames Waterway manager for the Environment Agency, acknowledged that boating had dwindled, yards were closing and river jobs were disappearing. Indeed, by the following year, traffic had fallen by 40 per cent from the levels reached in the 1970s, while the number of registered private boats had reduced by 25 per cent. The decline led to the creation of the River Thames Alliance, which consisted of various stakeholders who came together to produce two comprehensive plans (covering 2006–11 and 2015–21 respectively) to encourage use of the waterway, as well as to manage it better.[10]

Motorised Day-Boats

Hobbs started operating steamboats in the 1890s and it is likely they were rented out with a skipper. At the turn of the century, a Thames guidebook recorded that the firm was about to construct a number of electric craft that it planned to rent out for £2 2s per day. In 1906, a further addition to the fleet was a 30-foot launch, *Rosetta* (now renamed *Victoria*), bought from Saunders.

The company applied for a petrol storing licence in 1910, and by the late 1920s it had six motor launches ranging from 30–50 feet in length, as well as electric and motor canoes. It is not clear how many of these would have been self-drive boats, although overnight craft were not offered until the late 1950s (see below).

A regular complaint about rental craft was reckless navigation by customers. In 1954, Hylton Cleaver complained to the *Evening Standard* about 'river spivs' who could take to the water and cause problems for other Thames users without any redress. These included the 'illiterate adolescent', 'road hog' and even 'someone barred from the highway for ever as a motorist'.[11] The waterway authorities did regularly press charges against river users, but he was right that policing the Thames was a considerable challenge, as only a tiny fraction of the many offences could be prosecuted. Sometimes it was not the handling of the boat that was the issue, but the behaviour of those on board. In 1984, Hobbs had to call the police to escort a woman from Twyford off a craft, as she was too drunk to walk, after a trip to the George and Dragon at Wargrave.

By 1970, the firm boasted twenty-six day-boats. In 2006, it added two Edwardian-style launches by purchasing Rivertime, a company from Oakley Court that specialised in self-drive and chauffeur-driven parties for up to twelve people. The covered vessels, which numbered five by 2019, bridged the gap between the larger passenger craft and the smaller open day-boats, and were used for hospitality during the Henley Regatta. In 2013, one such craft was used by John McDermott, who wrote about his experience in the *Financial Times*.[12] In the same year, six Dutch-built Bullit 660 craft, worth £45,000 each, were added to the fleet. The craft had been used in the 2012 London Olympics to carry VIPs from central London to Stratford and could transport up to twelve people (or ten with a chauffeur). In 2018, one such 'Olympic class' boat was used in an episode on their YouTube channel by reality television stars Oliver Proudlock and Emma-Lou Connolly.

In 2014, a new type of boating experience was launched called the Henley Boat Club. The service was marketed to those who wanted the occasional use of luxury craft, but without the hassle and cost of buying, maintaining and mooring them. It was initially launched with the Olympic boats, but the range was subsequently expanded to include other day-boats, as well as the Linssen (overnight) cruisers. A range of packages was offered from the use of craft on a small number of days per year, to ones that included a boat at premium events, such as the Henley Festival or Royal Regatta. The initiative provided customers with a more exclusive experience, while it also generated a guaranteed income for the firm.

By 2019, the overall hire fleet numbered fifty-six craft – forty-two of which were motorboats – and they included Edwardian-style launches, Olympic, Antaris (that could carry four to twelve passengers), Pilot (four to twelve people) and Pearly class boats (up to four passengers), as well as an Alfrastreet 23 (that could accommodate up to eight) and rowing boats (that could carry three to five people).

Edwardian-style Launch
Lily-Anna, one of the firm's 31-foot Edwardian-style launches. (© Hobbs of Henley)

Olympic Class Boat
Argent One, approaching the regatta course, is an Olympic class boat that was used to transport dignitaries from central London to Stratford during the London 2012 Olympics. (© Sue Milton of www.thames-cards.co.uk)

Weather

The day-boat market relied heavily on casual customers, who, in turn, were influenced by the weather. The overall success of that part of the business was, therefore, largely determined by what the conditions were like at peak times, such as on the weekends, during school holidays and when special events were being held. In the 1950s, the firm started to report on the weather at its Annual General Meeting, as a way of explaining the financial results of the year. A particularly bad summer, like that of 1985, not only impacted small boat hire, but also other areas of the business, like fuel sales and chandlery purchases. It could also have a longer-term impact, as it might make customers think twice about travelling on the Thames the following year. That occurred in 1958, when poor rental figures were blamed on the previous summer. Two bad seasons in a row could be especially damaging, such as in 1963 and 1964, although fortunately they were followed by a number of better years.

A more serious hazard associated with wet weather was flooding. Riverside properties were often threatened by rising water levels in the colder months when boats were not being rented out (see chapter 5), but persistent heavy rain in the summer could have a devastating impact on trade. As the weirs of the locks had to be opened up more to flush the additional water through, the flow of the Thames could get sufficiently swift to make it unsafe for unpowered vessels – or sometimes all craft – to navigate. In 1968, for example, downpours prevented the firm from renting out craft on two different weeks in July with Dick Hobbs commenting that he had never seen such a fast current. Moreover, the major summer flood of 2007 had a very damaging impact on many Thames boat firms.

Conversely, good weather could transform the fortunes of the business with the firm enjoying a number of hot summers in the 1990s. In July 1994, for example, the company reported that bookings were up 20–25 per cent as the temperatures had soared. The following year a long, hot summer produced takings that were 10 per cent up on the previous year, while in 1997 the warm weather caused a 'massive increase in pleasure boat bookings'.[13]

Motorised Overnight Boats

One development that became popular in the interwar period was 'marine caravanning'. Although a motor cruiser club for private boats was established in Henley in 1936, it was not until 1958 that Hobbs entered the market, when Tony was assigned to build up a fleet. He commissioned *Girl Pat*, a 24-foot craft, which was the first of seven cabin cruisers that the firm constructed (with the fleet eventually numbering ten, through the purchase of others). Although this was relatively late for entering the market, the decision was partly inspired by the firm joining other operators in the Thames Hire Cruiser Association (founded in 1955). Hobbs was initially one of the smallest partners; by 1961 it only had a couple of two-berth craft and one six-berth boat, compared to the dominant Maid Line Cruisers of Thames Ditton, which had forty-seven vessels. The cabin cruisers were initially a great success; as the overheads were relatively low, they could be used for a long period (twenty-five to twenty-eight weeks per season), and they tended to be pre-booked. The latter was important, as the income offset some of the effects of bad summers. In 1959, for example, the directors noted that the new hire cruiser had compensated for what was otherwise 'a very poor year'.

The third craft the firm made was *Girl Marian* in 1961, a larger 35-foot craft that was the widest built at the Station Road yard (11 feet). It could sleep six on board and was named after the firm's early passenger boat (see chapter 4). After the launching of *Girl Lutena*, a 37-foot seven-berth cruiser christened by Jackie Hobbs in 1968, the company declared that it was cheap to run with the fuel costing 1s 3d an hour.

In 1961, the Association even produced its own *Thames Cruising Guide* for these 'friendly craft', which included instructions on how to cast off, hints on the river (written by Dick Hobbs), maps of the Thames, information about sights of interest, and advice on the provisions that were needed. When it came to clothing it suggested that 'informality is the by-word' as 'comfort counts more on a cruise than fashion', while it assured punters that you did not need to 'make-do', when it came to cooking with recommended dishes including grapefruit, scallops, and fish and chips. 'Galley gruel' (leftovers) could be eaten at the end of a trip.

Although the Association declared that such craft did not require 'high nautical skill' to handle, there were concerns among river users about their safety, because of the number of fires that occurred on them. In 1953, for example, Tony had to run down the towpath to call for assistance after *White Merlin*, a private craft moored near Phyllis Court, exploded and badly burned three men. In a single week in 1973, Hobbs experienced two such incidents. The first destroyed *Girl Pat* near Shifford Lock; the second involved an explosion after the firm had replaced the exhaust of a private craft. The latter forced an employee, Ivan Gardiner, to jump into the river off the craft and caused a 100-foot funnel of black smoke. As both incidents were reported in the *Henley Standard*, Tony wrote to the newspaper to point out that the fire on the private craft was not caused by the repair work, that the business had been hiring out motorised craft since the end the nineteenth century, and that the incident with *Girl Pat* was the first of its kind. The latter was replaced with *Pembrey*, a craft bought for £2,300 (partly funded by an insurance claim), and another, *Le Sabot*, was bought for £1,800. The firm's craft continued to have a good safety record, but issues with private vessels persisted. In 1976, again, Hobbs pointed out that a fire that broke out on a boat was

Six Cabin Cruisers

Six photographs of cabin cruisers. Clockwise from top right: *Le Sabot* (with the Hobbs family on board), *Girl Melanie*, *Girl Pat* (the first cabin cruiser) next to *Girl Jean*, *Girl Marian* being constructed and going into the slipway across the pathway, and *Girl Marian* (II) being delivered. (© Hobbs of Henley)

Midsomer
Midsomer, a Linssen 36.9 Grand Sturdy named after the TV show *Midsomer Murders*, was launched in 2015 by Sir Steve Redgrave. (© Hobbs of Henley)

unrelated to the work it had done (refuelling), while in 1997 and 2009 staff members helped out after explosions at the company's moorings. The later incident involved Ollie Johnson, a former employee, and Dominic Hook, the skipper of *Waterman*, coming to the assistance of a man trapped in the saloon by the blast, as well as towing away nearby craft to prevent further damage.

The number of incidents on the river as a whole was partly a reflection of the craft's popularity. Unlike many Association members, Hobbs chose not to ally with Hoseasons in the 1970s, which used television advertising to bring in a great deal of business to seventeen Thames operators. Instead, it entered into an advertising agreement with Boat Enquiries Ltd, an Oxford-based firm.

A boom in affordable package holidays and mounting running costs for cabin cruisers decimated the market in the 1980s. The number of such craft on the river fell from just over 800 at the start of the decade to just over 300 by the end of it. Although Tony mentioned the problem of rising registration fees to the *Henley Standard* on more than one occasion, in 1990 Hobbs followed some other companies by bowing out of the market. The decision was influenced by the recession, at a time when the firm was focusing more on its passenger boats (see chapter 4).

That was not the end of the story, however. Two decades later the firm reintroduced cruisers, but this time at the luxury end of the market ('head-turners', as Jonathan termed them). After being approached by the Dutch firm Linssen at the London Boat Show in 2013, Hobbs became the exclusive UK charter agent for the firm. It purchased a 34.9 Grand Sturdy

(*Jacqueline IV*), which was subsequently added to the fleet of the Henley Boat Club. This was followed two years later by a 36.9 model, which was launched by the rower Sir Steve Redgrave and was named *Midsomer*, after the television series *Midsomer Murders* that was filmed in the area.[14]

Final Thoughts

The Hobbs family has provided boats for hire in Henley since the middle of the Victorian period and, over the years, it has rented out vessels to hundreds of thousands of people, including many famous clients. In the second half of the twentieth century, these included local resident George Harrison, astrologer Russell Grant, and even Formula One champion Emerson Fittipaldi, whose experience on the sedate Pearly boats could not have been further removed from his day job. A career highlight for employee Peter Herbert was taking Hollywood stars Oliver Reed, Maggie Smith and Charlton Heston out on a cabin cruiser, while Tony Hobbs recalled Gene Kelly and Peggy Lee also using the firm's services.

The company had to remain flexible by continually modifying its fleet according to the changing flights of fashion. Although the introduction of pre-booked services helped to maintain a steadier cash flow, this side of the business was always heavily influenced by the weather. Furthermore, its overall success hinged on the revenue produced at peak times, such as during the main rowing events.

Chapter 2

Rowing and Other Recreations

Henley-on-Thames! What a name to conjure up visions of ambition or triumph to the oarsmen ... spurring each artist that beholds it to the immediate grasp of palette and brush to add his tribute to the charms of the scenery...

Emily Climenson, 1896[1]

The firm may have forged its reputation by renting out pleasure boats, but like many other Thames businesses in the town, its fortunes were heavily influenced by the sport of rowing. Yet, the Hobbs family also played its own part in developing the activity that came to define the essence of Henley.

Rowing: Competing

As they grew up overlooking the regatta course, it is perhaps unsurprising that a number of Harry Hobbs' sons became rowers. As was often the case, many of them graduated from coxing boats in their teenage years to becoming oarsmen. Although they were able to participate in the town's vibrant rowing scene, they embraced the sport at the end of the great era of professional rowing (1830–80), after which prohibitive legislation began to marginalise non-amateurs from many contests.

It was his younger brother, Arthur, who enjoyed the longest and most illustrious career. His Henley United Rowing Club crew of John Arlett, Harry Godley, Bert Ward and Harry Vaughan (cox) were said to have enjoyed 'so many victories' in their careers, including being undefeated for a whole season. John Arlett, the son of a publican from another notable Henley boating business, enjoyed a successful rowing and coaching career, which included training the Wiener Ruderklub Donau in Austria for the (aborted) 1916 Olympics. Arthur and John continued to compete together in a Senior Four crew that included Walter Parrott from a third boating firm, as well as Tom Arlett (John's younger brother). The river families knew each other well and often participated in fun events too, such as in 1913, when Arthur and Walter Parrott lost the 'tilting of canoes event' at the Watermen's and Fishermen's Regatta.

Two of the younger Hobbs brothers, Ernest and Frederick, also both competed for Henley United Rowing Club in the early Edwardian period, as did Bill's sons Dick and Reginald later on. Dick's son Tony continued the tradition by coxing for Henley Rowing Club in 1946 and was deemed a 'very valuable asset' because of his knowledge of boats and the river. At the junior level, he often rowed with Jack Arlett, and enjoyed some local success, such as winning the boys pair-oared race (with D. F. Steptoe) at the Wargrave and Shiplake Regatta of 1947, coming second at the junior sculling races at both Kingston and Molesey regattas in 1951 and winning the Senior Sculls at Henley Rowing Club's Regatta of 1953. The *Henley and South Oxfordshire Standard* claimed his greatest achievement was coming twentieth out of fifty-six competitors at the Head of the River sculling race at Putney in 1954, because he finished seven seconds ahead of Tony Fox, the reigning amateur champion, who had won the Diamond Sculls the previous year. The baton was handed down to his son, Jonathan, who rowed for the Oratory School, including at the Special Race for Schools at the Henley Royal Regatta from 1987–89, before doing a season competing in various regattas for Henley Rowing Club.[2]

Rowing: Organising

As well as being keen oarsmen, some of the Hobbs went on to serve in an organisational capacity. Many early rowing clubs were established in waterside pubs and, in 1887, Bill and Arthur were among fifty people who met in the Little White Hart to set up Henley United Rowing Club. The crews wore black and white and the training times were 6–8 a.m. and 5–9 p.m., except on Saturdays and Bank Holidays, when the boats were available all day. Bill became Deputy Captain of the club and Ernest Hobbs was added to the committee in 1893. Furthermore, Arthur became Honorary Secretary of the Henley Watermen's and Fishermen's Regatta (with Archibald Brakspear as the chairman) and Bill helped to organise the Olympic Regatta of 1908. The latter's grandson, Tony, became an Honorary Trustee of the Henley Town and Visitor's Regatta.

The family also often served in various official capacities during contests, such as being starters, judges or umpires – and sometimes umpire launch drivers – while they also assisted with fundraising events. From the early twentieth century onwards, the firm also constructed the Henley Regatta course.[3]

Rowing: Building the Henley Royal Regatta Course

Hobbs started constructing the Henley Royal Regatta course in 1919, after the man who was assigned to the task (described in chapter 7) let the committee down. Tom Steward, who organised the event, managed to persuade Hobbs to buy the equipment and take on the workmen who had already done the job for years.[4] After completing their regatta duties, the piling gang were used for a wide range of different construction projects, including the steel sheeting of riverbanks, as well as building landing stages, mooring sites and footbridges. This was an important side of the business as it produced a large proportion of the turnover, as well as revenue outside of the summer months. The firm continued the undertaking until 1988, when it decided to stop the highly labour-intensive work that could be adversely affected by flooding in the winter. The equipment used to build the course was sold to the Henley Royal Regatta, which retained the services of John Fenn, who continued to manage the business.

Piling Gang
The Hobbs piling gang. The firm was responsible for building the Henley Regatta course from 1919 to 1988, as well as constructing many landing stages and bridges. The image on the left shows the previous method of driving in the piles. (© Hobbs of Henley)

Rowing: Umpire and Coaching Launches

Hobbs probably did not have any motorised craft until the 1890s, but one of its first passenger boats, *Ghoorka*, was certainly fast enough for coaching (see below), as Harcourt Gold utilised it during Leander's training for the Henley Regatta of 1903. Nevertheless, it was not until 1912 that Hobbs gained the contract to provide the official umpire launches for the event (see chapter 3). Furthermore, a 27-foot steam-powered canoe called *Scotia* (renamed *Toppings*), built by the firm in 1928 and used in its hire fleet, was one of three (the others being *Olive* and *Water Lily*) that Hobbs fitted out with petrol engines and sold to Oxford University Boat Club in 1953, for use as coaching craft.[5] The company still has a

Consuta II
Consuta II was used to ferry the GB rowing team to Dorney Lake during the 2012 London Olympics. (© Hobbs of Henley)

significant contract with the Henley Royal Regatta to provide twelve drivers for the annual event: six highly skilled watermen for the umpire launches and six to operate the ferries.

Rowing: Transportation

The firm still provides a fleet of eight craft for the Henley Regatta. Six Pilot boats are used to transport passengers from the Steward's Enclosure to the Fawley Meadows Hospitality Centre, while *Winchat* and *Crossbill* carry officials up and down the course. Furthermore, in 2012, Hobbs provided the official transportation service for the GB rowing team at the London Olympics. The company beat many other Thames businesses to the prestigious contract, which involved using *Consuta II* and two Edwardian-style launches to ferry personnel from Oakley Court to Dorney Lake. In the process, Darren Martin, the skipper of the former, befriended a number of the competitors.[6]

Rowing: Building Racing Boats

The family may have had close links with the rowing scene, but unlike some professional oarsmen, they probably did not compete in boats they had built. Indeed, the family may not have constructed *any* type of boat initially (see chapter 3), when the racing boat market was already dominated by specialist firms elsewhere, like Clasper, Rough, and Swaddle and Winship. Henley businesses did not reach the pinnacle of the field, although Arlett and Glyn Locke enjoyed some success in the 1920s and 1980s respectively.

Hobbs did have some faster craft. In 1895, Hugh Gardner used one in a successful wager to row 30 miles in six hours. (Such speed contests were not uncommon and, in 1824, six guardsmen managed to row from Oxford to London in fifteen hours twenty-five minutes, a record that was not beaten until 1971.) Gardner had intended to use a boat from Staines, but was forced to transfer to one from Hobbs when there was a problem with his chosen craft. He reached Penton Hook in five hours and fifty minutes (with an hour allowed for lunch), followed by spectators on board *Ghoorka*, the boat on which he made the bet. The craft he used may not necessarily have been Hobbs-built, but the gig four presented by the firm to Henley United Rowing Club in 1902 probably was. It was designed to help young people start to row, before they graduated onto the faster racing craft.[7]

Rowing: Storage

A constant challenge for rowing clubs was the housing of boats and Hobbs played its part in helping some of them. Although the firm turned down a request in 1884 to accommodate vessels for Henley Rowing Club in its new yard – as did competitors Johnson and Peacey – some space was subsequently found, as it was receiving £25 a year for the service by the turn of the century. The Upper Thames Skiff Club was another to use the Hobbs facilities, as the firm's Shiplake yard was its headquarters in 1908. In 1970, the company also offered Henley Rowing Club use of a site in the same location, when it was seeking alternative premises.

Other Types of Boating

The business also formed connections with other boat clubs. In 1929, Henley Sailing Club, based at Shiplake, presented Ernest with a silver salver, as an anniversary gift in recognition of all the 'little acts of kindness' that he had shown them. In the twenty-first century, Hobbs provided support for the fundraising initiatives of many local groups, including the Henley Dragons, a dragon boat club formed in 1991.[8]

Swimming

The family also had involvement with another form of aquatic leisure: swimming. In 1914, Cyril Hobbs beat all the other students, including his older cousin, Dick, who came second, to win the Henley Grammar School's Phyllis Challenge Cup. The contest involved sculling, diving, life-saving and swimming – the latter from Hobbs' boathouse to the Manor Garden Lawn.

Bill Hobbs was also involved in the discussions that led to the bathing place at Solomon's Hatch (off the Wargrave Road) being turned into a council-run facility in the early twentieth century. Large numbers visited the site, including 2,725 people over the August Bank Holiday weekend of 1933 (a number equivalent to approximately 40 per cent of the town's population).

The popularity of swimming in the interwar period also raised the question of what was considered appropriate attire. In 1929 and 1934, the *Henley and South Oxfordshire Standard* reported on what it considered to be the 'disgusting' and 'indecent' state of semi-nude bathers in the river.

Nor was this discussion just confined to swimming; in 1934 the Thames Conservancy tried to introduce a by-law that required those on boats to be clothed appropriately when passing through the locks. The idea was rejected by Leslie Hore-Belisha, the Minister of Transport, however. He said applying the rule would be impractical, as the general fashion had shifted from the exquisite outfits of the Victorian and Edwardian times to a trend of wearing 'as little as possible'.[9]

Football

The family also developed close links with the sport of football. Bill Hobbs was not able to play on a Saturday afternoon because of work commitments and, therefore, at one point he played with other local tradesmen on a Wednesday afternoon. It is not clear what team that was for, but both Arthur and Ernest played for Henley Football Club in the 1880s. They were also involved with its merger with Rovers FC in 1896, after which the former became secretary and the latter deputy chairman. Soon afterwards all of the brothers temporarily withdrew from the club, under pressure from their father, after Frederick suffered a particularly nasty compound fracture to his right leg during a game against Clerkenwell.

Arthur subsequently returned to the committee and the family's association with the club continued with Dick, who overcame an operation on his toes in 1919, to become the club's captain and top scorer for two seasons running (1919/20 and 1920/21). A particular highlight was playing in front of 3,000 people at the White House Ground in Oxford in the final of the Oxfordshire Senior Cup, which Henley lost 2-1 (to Banbury Britannia works). Although Dick retired from playing in his early twenties, possibly because of work commitments, in the 1930s he occasionally played for the Old Henleiensians (for former Henley Grammar School boys) alongside his best man, Len Walden, and cousins Cyril (who had been a goalkeeper for the YMCA team) and Eddie. He became chairman of the club in the early 1930s and was Honorary Secretary for twelve seasons, as well as head of Henley Charity Football Competitions. He also held senior positions at the Football Association, as South Oxfordshire's councillor from 1933, and later vice president of Oxfordshire.

The family's association with football continued into the twenty-first century with Jonathan's daughter, Bella, top scorer for Wargrave Girls FC in 2014. Two years later, the firm donated a boat for use by Henley Town FC in a special fundraising party that raised £1,200 for the club.[10]

Rugby

Although his father was a footballing man, Tony became a rugby player who enjoyed a long career for Old Henleiensians, the team that became Henley Rugby Football Club in 1963. He was a wing-forward and kicker from the late 1950s onwards, as well as club captain for a then record of three years in a row. He won the club's annual kicking competition in 1961 and played in the early games against Le Havre, which became an annual fixture. His father, Dick, who became an avid supporter, served as vice president of the club in the late 1960s, while Tony himself later became president. They also helped out with fundraising, such as in 1968, when the firm won the 'capsize by falling out of the boat contest' at the club's annual donkey derby. Furthermore, there is still a 'Hobbs Bar' at the Dry Leys ground that was named after the family, because they donated money towards a major refurbishment of the clubhouse in 2015.

The Old Henleiensians Rugby Team, 1962–3
The Old Henleiensians rugby team for former Grammar School boys (just before it was renamed Henley Rugby Football Club) with captain Tony Hobbs holding the ball. (© Reproduced by permission of the *Henley Standard* from 17 May 1963)

Other Sports

The Hobbs were involved with other sports too. Cyril was a member of Henley Rifle Club in the early 1930s, before joining Trinity Rifle Club at the end of the decade. Although he tended to be in the B side for the former, he won the club's Tyro Cup in 1933, and was selected for the twenty-strong county side in 1936.

Tony Hobbs was also an avid runner who entered a number of international marathons. For many years he was in charge of Henley's half marathon, a fundraising event for the RNLI he helped to launch in 1982. He was also involved in some more informal contests, such as in 1981, when he and Jackie represented Peppard in a bar billiards competition against local rivals, Wargrave.[11]

Other Activities

The Hobbs family were not only connected with the sporting life of Henley, but they were also active in the local social scene. They often participated in fundraising events, such as whist drives for good causes. On Shrove Tuesday in 1904, they attended a fancy-dress 'calico' ball. Bill went in Georgian costume, his wife, Ada, went as a brush and palette, Frederick and Edith went in boating attire, Ernest went as a naval officer, and their younger sisters, Ethel and Eveline, went as Grace Darling and a country girl respectively.

One can also get a sense of the frivolity at some of the musical events, like the Ancient Order of Druid's outing to the George and Dragon at Wargrave in 1908, during which many 'capital songs' were performed, including a rendition of 'Kitty Tyrrell' by Harry. They were certainly a musical family, as Arthur sometimes sang at Druid events, Bill became vice president of the Henley Royal Amateur Operatic and Dramatic Society, and Ernest was on the committee of the Henley Musical Society. The next generation was also involved in the performing arts, as Cassie was an accomplished pianist who played at many local events. At a Young Helpers League fete at Northfield House in 1910, she orchestrated the performances of the children, including her younger siblings, Margie and Dick, who were Red Riding Hood and Boy Blue respectively. The latter (and with his future wife, Edith) went on to perform for the Henley Royal Amateur Operatic and Dramatic Society.[12]

Final Thoughts

Although the idea had been suggested as early as the 1930s, it was not until 1998 that Henley had a permanent River and Rowing Museum to showcase the town's long tradition of aquatic leisure. Although the famous figures of the sport were rightfully honoured in it, as this chapter has shown, the Hobbs family made its own important contribution to the activity, even though much of it was behind the scenes. Furthermore, many well-known Olympic rowers have used the firm's services, including Alex Gregory and the other GB team members ferried to Dorney Lake in 2012, and those with boats moored in Henley, like Sir Steve Redgrave, Matthew Pinsent and James Cracknell. Yet for many decades the business was viewed predominantly as a boatbuilding firm, as we see in the next chapter.

Chapter 3

Boatbuilding

Henley is not much given to manufactures, except beer and boats… It is only right that a town so adapted to such possibilities of aquatic exercise and sport should produce good river craft.

Emily Climenson, 1896[1]

In her extensive guide to Henley of 1896, Emily Climenson suggested that pleasure boats had only been 'native built', i.e. constructed in the town, for a short period. It is not clear when Hobbs began building craft, but the *Victoria County History* argues that Harry, who was a carpenter, may not have done so until new boathouses were constructed *c*. 1884. Two other sources support this contention, although the dating differs slightly. One is Kelly's trade directory; it was not until the 1887 edition that he was listed as a 'ship and general boat builder'. The other was a Thames guide published in 1899, which suggested that the firm started constructing craft twenty years earlier (presumably approximately) in a 'small yard with one boat'.[2] This also matches the general trend in Henley, as the number of boatbuilders recorded in the census rose from five in 1881 to fifteen a decade later, during the 'golden age of the Thames' (see chapter 1).

By the later date, Harry was offering to produce the more technical steam launches, although in 1893 he almost lost some of his equipment in an attempted robbery. Upon entering his boathouse, he startled a man, John Donald, who dropped the footsquare and tenon saw he was holding. Harry, who had experience of dealing with difficult customers at the pub (see chapter 5), got hold of the thief's collar and handed him to the police. At the trial, he made it clear that he did not want to press charges against the man, who had a large family depending on him, but a sentence of seven days' hard labour was meted out to the miscreant.

By the end of the century his firm was advertising that it could build any type of (small) Thames craft, while guaranteeing the best of materials and workmanship. There are no records that show how many craft Hobbs constructed in the early years, but by the beginning of the twentieth century the output was thought to have been approximately twenty to thirty per annum, which would have been steady work for a smallish firm. Demand would naturally have fluctuated during the year with the springtime being the busiest, when customers ordered craft for the summer season. Indeed, in 1904, an article in the *Daily Telegraph* noted that around Whitsuntide the boatbuilders of Henley were 'working nearly night and day to keep pace with the higher demand', because of all of the patronage on the river.[3]

It is thought that around that time the firm was largely building skiffs and punts, which had both become popular at the end of the previous century. The former had replaced the heavier and more cumbersome gig, while the design changes that helped popularise the

Emgee
Emgee, a dinghy built by Hobbs *c.* 1900, is now on display at the River and Rowing Museum.
(© River and Rowing Museum, Henley-on-Thames)

A 25-FT. PETROL MOTOR CANOE.

A very highly-finished and efficient Boat, having the advantage over the Electric Canoe of unlimited radius.   Suitable for 5 persons.   Runs comfortably at 8 Knots with a 2 Cylinder "Watermota."

Canoe
A canoe built by Hobbs in the 1920s. (© Hobbs of Henley)

latter were a narrowing of the beam (making them more manoeuvrable), construction from tropical hardwoods (making them more attractive) and, most importantly, the introduction of saloon seating in the centre (making them more sociable).[4] Dinghies were also constructed by Hobbs at that time and one of them, *Emgee* (*c.* 1900), is displayed at the River and Rowing Museum.

Canoes were also very popular, partly thanks to the legacy of John MacGregor (1825–92), an explorer whose accounts of his travels on board *Rob Roy* (a kayak built by Searle of Stangate) became bestsellers in the late 1860s. From the 1890s onwards, many Thames firms imported them from Canada, and it is possible that Hobbs might have done so too. Yet many were constructed in-house, including *Sandpiper* (renamed *Steampiper*), a 24-foot canoe that was originally electric and was believed to be in a batch of six made in 1912. Others built by Hobbs include *Céomé*, a 29-foot 6-inch steam-powered craft (built in 1921), *Tadpole* (renamed *Nyra*), a 27-foot 2-inch steam craft (1923) and *Unktahee* (renamed *Minnie Shoo Shoo*), a 27-foot 4-inch motor canoe (*c.* 1926), as well as three used later as coaching craft for rowers at Oxford University in the 1950s (see chapter 2). In the mid-1920s, the cost of a 25-foot model made from mahogany on oak with a two-cylinder Watermota unit and Langdon reverse gear was £275. Hobbs had clearly made a name for itself by building such craft, as in 1922 the *Daily Telegraph* declared that electric canoes, as well as electric and motor launches, were the 'famous firm's specialties', in addition to its umpire launches (see below). The paper also reported that the firm was exporting them, as it said that they were being 'built for use on rivers in various parts of the world'.

AUX CRUISER, 25ft. × 8ft., × 1ft. 6in.

Designed and built with a view to meet the demand of those of limited means. The upkeep of this Boat is negligible, while it has all the advantages of a foating home, and the independence which cannot be obtained on a Houseboat. The mechanical power, which is installed under the floor in the aft well, is a "Saunders" 2 Cylinder Unit. On her trials she attained a speed, with motor only, of 5 Knots.

Aux Cruiser
A 25-foot aux cruiser constructed by Hobbs in 1924. (© Hobbs of Henley)

" MONTREAL."

A 50-FT. ESTUARY & BROADS CRUISER, built in 1920.

The main cabin is 20 feet in length and comprises 2 Berths, Sideboard, Wardrobe, Bathroom and Lavatory Accommodation. A speed of 10 Knots is obtained with a 30-H.P. 6 Cylinder "Wolseley" Marine Engine.

Montreal
Montreal, a 50-foot estuary and broads cruiser built by Hobbs in 1920. (© Hobbs of Henley)

Two unusual craft Hobbs constructed around this time were *Montreal*, a 50-foot estuary and broads cruiser (1920), and a 25-foot aux cruiser. The latter, which was taken to the Marine and Small Craft Exhibition of 1924, had a mainmast that could be easily lowered to go through bridges and was marketed as meeting the demand of those with limited means, by being a moveable houseboat. It was priced at £450 and its construction led to Hobbs subsequently claiming to be a yacht builder.

Until the acquisition of the Springfield Yard in 1911, the firm was probably only building craft out of wood. Furthermore, like many other boatbuilders, it relied upon external companies to provide the engines. It also occasionally sold them second hand for clients. In 1924, one such transaction ended up in a legal dispute resulting in a customer receiving damages for being supplied with a faulty item, having already bought a launch from the Springfield works.[5]

It was around that time that Hobbs began to build slipper launches, a craft often associated with John Andrews, whose firm started constructing them prior to the First World War. Some were intended for the rental market and were built to a simpler design, like the 24-foot *Impey* (1933), but others, like the 30-foot *Carry Me Back* (1937) were made to a very high standard. Among the many constructed by the firm were the 30-foot *Omrah* (1934), 27-foot *Foxglove* (1937) and 25-foot *Rowena* – the latter being used by Hobbs for special events into the twenty-first century. In 2006, one of the firm's slipper launches was replicated by a Dutch firm and named *Larkspur*.

A notable motor boat that was not a slipper launch was *Cachalot* (renamed *Belle Epoque*), a 30-foot gentleman's launch, built in 1937 for Mr Knight of Henley, the head of the soap dynasty. Another was *Elsie*, a craft that won an award at the 1987 traditional boat show. Constructed in 1913 (to a Saunders design), it was used by the Red Cross during the First World War to give convalescing soldiers trips on the river.

Despite the need for vessels in the two World Wars, the firm does not appear to have built any craft for the Admiralty. Even in the Second World War, when some Henley businesses produced parts for aeroplanes, the boathouses of Hobbs were relatively quiet, including the Springfield yard at Goring, which was used for storing craft. The firm did provide the Royal Marines with canoes from its rental fleet though.

After the Springfield site was sold in 1949, the firm constructed boats from the Station Road yard in Henley. In 1958, for example, Tony oversaw the building of *Girl Pat*, the first of seven cabin cruisers produced by Hobbs. Five years later, a similar boat was constructed for a private client; *Knee Deep* (1963) was a 32-foot craft that was designed by Fred Cooper, who had been responsible for Sir Malcolm Campbell's record-breaking *Bluebird*. It was not built for speed, but came with various mod-cons, including a gas cooker and refrigerator, as well as an 'eye-catching dashboard with 12 gauges'. Other craft built in the early 1960s included a 58-foot canal cruiser and *Mabella II*, a classic Italian-style open launch.

By the middle of the decade, however, the boatbuilding side of the business was suffering, because of a number of bad summers and the introduction of fibreglass construction, which had a devastating impact on wooden craftsmanship across the country. Some firms sought to keep the traditional methods alive, most notably Peter Freebody of Hurley, but the last craft built by Hobbs was *Girl Lutena* in 1968. After that point the company moved to a model of being agents for other suppliers with many products sold through the chandlery.[6]

Chandlery

In 1965, when the boatbuilding side of the business was winding down, Hobbs Marine Store Ltd was launched, which was a separate company owned by Tony and Jackie Hobbs. The enterprise, which revolved around the sale of craft and outboard engines, was run by Ray Gardiner, who built up the trade by developing relationships with many different clients and suppliers. The firm acted as agents for lots of companies, such as Fletcher, Windboats, Evinrude and Seagull in 1968, as well as, subsequently, Chrysler, Honda and Fairline. For a short period Gardiner supplied every craft sold directly through Shetland boats, which amounted to around thirty per year in the 1980s. Boats had to be delivered all around the country – sometimes at short notice – and one unusual order involved taking a craft to Heathrow, which was put on a jumbo jet for a client in the Middle East. A huge range of people used what was marketed in the nineties as 'the best stocked chandlery', but it was a nucleus of individuals that kept it going. It also enjoyed patronage from a number of famous clients, including musicians like Vince Hill, Barrie Barlow (of Jethro Tull) and Jay Kay (of Jamiroquai), footballers like Ray Clemence, as well as other notable local luminaries such as Jeremy Paxman.

On a number of occasions, Gardiner won trips to the United States from the Outboard Motor Corporation for being one of the top three salespeople in the country. He sold 102 in his last year of trading, although the figure had previously been much higher.

The chandlery was a particularly important part of the business, because it brought in further longer-term sources of revenue. If a powered boat was sold, for example, the customer would need to buy an engine for it, and, once it was operational, often a place was required to keep it. Indeed, Hobbs managed to fill up its own moorings with many of the craft that were sold at the chandlery. Other ongoing services were then needed, such as providing fuel or equipment, or using the boatyard for maintenance, repair or storage. Although the chandlery diversified over time and even embraced a mail-order service, in the twenty-first century it began to be impacted by online sales. It was eventually closed in 2008, because Hobbs wanted to develop the site into a restaurant.[7]

Slipper Launches
Omrah, an elegant 30-foot slipper launch constructed by Hobbs in 1934 (left), alongside *Cygnet 11*, a more conventional slipper launch built by Andrews in 1932. (© Rupert Stevens)

Enchantress
Princesses Elizabeth and Margaret attending the Henley Royal Regatta in 1946 on the umpire launch *Enchantress* (built in 1913). The skipper is Laurie Truss. Tony Hobbs is behind him, and Dick Hobbs is holding the rope. (© Reproduced by permission of the *Henley Standard*)

Umpire Launches

Steamboats were first used as umpire launches at the Henley Royal Regatta in 1869, but it was not until 1912 that Hobbs gained the contract to start providing the vessels. The company was used because it had bought the Springfield yard of Sam Saunders, the boatbuilder who had revolutionised the design of such craft. His *Consuta* (1898), which could achieve a speed of 27.5 knots, was constructed with a tunnel stern to produce less wash and its innovative hull was particularly light, as it was made from four laminations sewn together with copper wire. It was used in an official capacity alongside a privately owned vessel called *Hibernia* (built in 1894), before another Saunders craft, *Maritana*, replaced it in 1905.

The arrangement with Hobbs was that it had to provide a petrol-powered craft for the regatta for £40 a year. *Enchantress* (1913), which was powered by an Ithad 45hp 6-cylinder engine, was the first to be built. It had the honour of carrying the royal party, including Princesses Elizabeth (the current Queen) and Margaret, in the first post-war Henley Regatta of 1946, and it was driven by road down to Putney for the 1957 Oxford-Cambridge University Boat Race. Tony and the Hobbs family retained a special affection for *Enchantress*, as it was used by the firm for decades, but its condition eventually deteriorated to such an extent that it was reluctantly sold in 2018.

The next to be built was *Magician* (1921), which was not a copper-stitched *Consuta* type, as the emergence of lighter and more powerful engines had rendered the laborious method of construction unnecessary. Propelled by an Austin Skipper 100, a 4-litre, 6-cylinder engine, it was used by the Prince of Wales at the 1921 Henley Royal Regatta. *Magician* also transported the kit for the BBC's first live outside radio broadcast of the Boat Race in 1927, which included a half-ton transmitter and four engineers to operate it. It continued to be used at Henley until 1994, before being sold two years later.

Magician was followed by *Amaryllis* in 1928, a 50-foot training launch owned by Cambridge University Boat Club. It was used by the light blues during the Boat Race and was kept by Hobbs for rental work, as well as for official duties at the Henley Regatta. It carried many dignitaries at the latter, including the Duke and Duchess of York (later George VI and Queen Consort Elizabeth) in 1931. In 2017, its long-time skipper, Daniel Wood, recalled one occasion when the craft was immobilised midstream as the Goldie crew was inspecting the university course in London. A gravel bag had to be cut from the propeller, but the anchor was difficult to retrieve as it had caught around the submerged axel of a Mini. *Amaryllis* also had the distinction of being the 'mother' of the modern generation of fibreglass umpire launches that were all produced from a mould taken from its hull. Although the subsequent boats (*Herakles, Argonaut, Ariadne* and *Ulysses*) were built in Norfolk from the 1990s onwards, the *Henley Standard* declared that their appearance ensured that they were still 'known affectionately in the rowing world as "Hobbs launches"'. *Amaryllis* was sold to a private buyer in 1996, but it was restored and continued to be used in an official capacity.

In 1952, having already supplied one to Cambridge, Hobbs built *Bosporos* for Oxford University Boat Club, which was the last of its umpire launches. As the Springfield yard had been sold, it had to be built in the first-floor boathouse at Station Road, in Henley, which posed a considerable challenge when it came to taking it out of the workshop. The craft, named after a Greek compound word meaning 'ox ford', was a gift from Lord Nuffield and was designed by W. Waight. 'Oxford's famous coaching launch', as the *Henley Standard* described it, was subsequently owned by the Henley Royal Regatta Stewards from 1980 to 1992, before being sold. A smaller craft of the firm's, *Arethusa* (1921), was also occasionally used in an official capacity from 1976 onwards, following restoration at Freebody's yard.

***Enchantress* with the Hobbs Family on Board, 2012**
The Hobbs family on board *Enchantress* (with Tony at the wheel) at the Queen's Diamond Jubilee
Tea Party, which was held at the Henley Business School in 2012. (© Hobbs of Henley)

Amaryllis* and *Enchantress
A number of small photographs showing the building and transporting of the umpire launches
Amaryllis (top left) and *Enchantress* (bottom right). (© Hobbs of Henley)

Magician
A private party on the umpire launch *Magician*, built in 1921. (© Hobbs of Henley)

Bosporos
The careful process of extracting the umpire launch *Bosporos* from the first-floor yard at Station Road in 1952. (© Hobbs of Henley)

The financial importance of the launches was confirmed by the directors of Hobbs in 1957, when they reported that a poor summer was compensated by the contracts the company had for 'all the main regattas of the Thames' (a season stretching from April to August). The craft also acted as small high-end passenger boats that were popular with clients. Yet, as they aged, they became increasingly expensive to maintain. In 1990, Tony Hobbs declared that they were 'loss leaders' that were 'totally uneconomic to run' and were only kept going because of 'tradition and sentiment'. Despite that, they were invaluable as a highly distinctive feature of Hobbs' workmanship and an important visual form of marketing (see chapter 4). They not only collectively carried huge numbers of VIPs over the years, but they were also in demand for television and film work. They were featured in a BBC Home Service programme in 1952, the musical *Half a Sixpence* in 1967, Channel 4's *Country Matters* in 1991, and BBC1's *Countryfile* in 2013.[8]

Passenger Boats

Although the umpire launches constructed by Hobbs could carry small parties, the firm did not build larger passenger boats. That was probably because there was limited demand for such craft and other businesses were already dominating the market. Indeed, the passenger boats used by Hobbs in the 1890s were built by Shepherd (see chapter 4), and even with the acquisition of the Springfield yard, which enabled vessels of up to around 75 feet to be built, the majority of those constructed there were between 30 feet and 50 feet in length. One that the firm built was *Margherita* (1922), a 40-foot craft similar in appearance to the umpire launches that could accommodate fifty passengers. It was bought by T. W. Hitchins and was used for trips between Bath and Bradford-on-Avon, as well as for party work.

Boatyard Services

As a prominent boatbuilder, Bill Hobbs was considered to be an authority on river craft. On two occasions (1895 and 1907) he was an expert witness in court cases about the disrepair of a houseboat, the second of which related to *Emmie*, a craft that sank after Albert Parrott had hired it to a customer. Indeed, maintaining large wooden boats was a considerable challenge and the number of such vessels on the river declined over the course of the twentieth century, as many of them succumbed to the water.

Hobbs did not initially put a great onus on repairs in its marketing, although it was advertising storage and varnishing services by 1898 and claimed to have a 'good slipway for hauling launches' by 1904. During the Second World War, it offered help with 'engine repairs, troubles and overhauls', and, by the end of the following decade, it advertised the repair and reconditioning of private craft.

The yards were also used for the fitting out of craft, such as when Hobbs did this for a small number of narrowboats in the 1970s, the hulls of which came from the Midlands. Private clients could also use the facilities and one couple, who had a fibreglass hull delivered to the Wargrave Road boathouse, were Mike and Trisha Crocker. In 1981, they realised a lifelong dream by setting sail around the world on board their 33-foot sloop *Nyn* ('not yet named'). Sadly, disaster struck in Trinidad early the next year, when an intruder overpowered them and murdered Mike, while Trisha and two visiting friends managed to swim to safety. The craft was brought back by HMS *Fearless* and returned to Henley, where Tony Hobbs had offered a mooring. Trisha, who was an American sculptor and psychotherapist, wrote *The Tear Vessel*, a novel informed by the experience, while the Crocker family, who had run a historic shoe-repairing business in the town, set up a foundation in Michael's name, to give young people the opportunity to go sailing.

The firm's yards were also used for the launching of many craft. One was *Zolander* in 1971, said to be one of the first steam-powered craft built on the river since the war. Ten years later, Tony Hobbs christened a new boat for Hephaistos School in Farley Hills, for use by those with physical disabilities.[9]

Final Thoughts

By 2019, Hobbs offered summer and annual moorings, winter and short-term storage (under cover or in the open), as well as fuel and water from Station Road. The repair of craft, including woodwork, fibreglass repairs, painting and varnishing, was handled by one side of the business, while various other services were devolved to external companies based at the firm's Wargrave Road yard. Launching and inboard engine services and repair were provided by G Mech Marine, a business that was lifting sixty to seventy craft every winter by 2013, while stern drive and outboard services, sales and spare parts were handled by Bluenine Marine.

Although the firm was never a major builder of craft, Hobbs-built vessels were ever-present at events that celebrated the river's history, like the annual traditional boat rally in Fawley Meadows (first organised by the River Thames Society in 1978). In 2012, *Amaryllis* was the sole craft connected with the business to feature in the Thames Jubilee Pageant (in the Historic and Service boats category), while the following year *Elsie* and *Enchantress* featured in Henley's own pageant to celebrate the sixtieth anniversary of the Queen's coronation. By that point, however, the firm was best known for its passenger boat services.

Chapter 4

Passenger Boats

Thousands of city men and women, youths and maidens, know this twentieth-century Eden. They adore it, they go there for the day, for the week-end, for the summer holidays... Henley is always beautiful. Here one sees the Thames in all of its glory.

Evening News, 1922[1]

Steamboat trips became popular in London in the early nineteenth century, but they were much slower to take off on the higher reaches of the waterway. One reason was the greater operating costs, as the locks limited the size of craft and you had to pay to pass through them. It was not until the 1880s that steamer services proliferated on the non-tidal Thames. In Henley, initially, craft from outside of the town had to be used by those wanting a river trip, such as in 1884, when Johnson and Peacey arranged for *Alaska* to take the Working Men's Institute from Henley to Windsor with Bill Hobbs assisting with the local navigation.

Tom Shepherd of the Red Lion was the early pioneer and market leader in the town, as he started running services in 1889 (see below). Yet rather than protecting his business, he did the neighbouring firm of Hobbs a considerable favour by building it two passenger boats, even though they were direct competition for his own vessels. The first was *Ghoorka*, a name that was possibly chosen by Bill, who was a military man (see chapter 6). The second boat, *Marian* (operated by Hobbs from 1892–1914), was a larger 50-foot craft that gained a passenger boat licence for up to seventy-three people (although it was subsequently reduced). It was certainly the flagship of the fleet, as early telegrams to the firm could be addressed to 'Marian, Henley'. Among the varied clientele *Marian* carried were the Young Men's Friendly Society (in 1893), a temperance party (1893), a 'novel' wedding party where everyone wore boating attire (1899), servants of the Three Elms who enjoyed a 'delightfully happy day' with a champagne lunch (1906), and employees of the newly built Joyce Grove from Nettlebed (1909).

It was not all plain sailing in the early years, however, as the Thames Conservancy regularly hauled up private individuals and operators for navigation offences. In 1894, Ernest Hobbs was summoned to answer charges of breaking the rules at the Goring and Streatley Regatta, although the case was dismissed, when it was judged that insufficient time had been allowed for launches to pass by the course. A much more serious incident occurred near Shiplake on 28 June 1909, when *Marian* collided heavily with the *Windsor Belle*, a passenger boat run by Arthur Jacobs of Windsor. The force was such that the former, which was hit on the bow, spun around completely in the water, while the latter, which was struck amidships, had its cabin ripped clean away. *Windsor Belle* remained in a wounded state for much of the season, causing Jacobs unsuccessfully to bring an action against the Henley firm for repairs (£42), loss of income (£20) and damages (£100). He claimed *Marian* had travelled at an excessive speed, while Hobbs maintained that the *Windsor Belle* did not have an adequate lookout, had not yielded to the craft travelling downstream and had made no attempt to pass port-side to port-side. Sampson Gomm, the seventeen-year-old skipper of *Windsor Belle*, and Henry Hooper, his counterpart on *Marian*, both claimed they had sounded their whistles first as they approached the point, but the latter reported that the former had admitted fault. William Russel, the engineer of the Hobbs boat, who had eased off at his skipper's behest, suggested the collision would have been averted had the other vessel done the same. Although both crews supported their own colleague's version of events, the deadlock was fortunately broken by a neutral witness, James Plant, the captain of the *Queen of England*, run by Maynard of Windsor. He testified that Gomm had admitted that he had not been at the wheel at the time of the incident because he was scrubbing down in the stern, but had asked him not to tell Mr Jacobs for fear of losing his job. That explained why the craft had not followed protocol, as another crew member had been at the helm. The *Windsor Belle*, which was beautifully restored in 1986, currently has a permanent mooring at Hobbs' Wargrave Road yard.

Marian was dispensed with around the time of the First World War and was thought to have later been used (and lost) in the Dunkirk evacuations. The firm did not completely leave the market, however, as the umpire launches were subsequently used for carrying small parties.[2]

Ferrying

Some of the early passenger boat trips were essentially ferry services between one location and another. In 1898, *Marian* was used by the Congregational Church in Henley to take 400 people up to Greenlands for the Sunday School's annual outing. The journey was sometimes far shorter, such as in 1902, when Hobbs lent an electric launch to Henley Swimming Club

Windsor Belle
The beautifully restored *Windsor Belle* (built in 1901) at its mooring at Hobbs' Wargrave Road yard in 2019. The craft was badly damaged in 1909 after a collision with Hobbs' passenger boat *Marian*. (© Simon Wenham)

Waterman
The 85-foot *Waterman* was bought by the firm in 2004. (© Hobbs of Henley)

to take the competitors from the lawn to the starting punt. Over a century later, the firm provided a similar service by transporting competitors during the Henley 'club to pub' swim (first held in 2014). Hobbs also occasionally offered its services free of charge when there were emergencies, such as in 2014, when it helped people across the river, after a chemical spillage near the Angel closed the bridge.

The firm also became the official ferry service provider for a number of major events, including the annual flower show at Fawley Court at the end of the nineteenth century (the journey costing 3*d*). Similarly, when a Grand Fete was held there in 1905, the business offered the same service, but this time charged 6*d* for a single trip and 9*d* for a return, as well as 6*d* for round trips to Hambleden Lock.

Hobbs was less able to provide such services when it stopped running passenger boats, but the smaller craft could still be used for short services. Yet, once the passenger boat fleet was restored and expanded (from the 1980s onwards), the firm was again able to transport larger numbers. Indeed, Hobbs' craft were used at many notable events in the twenty-first century, including the Henley Regatta, the Fringe and Rewind Festivals, and the Thames Traditional Boat Festival. A particular prestigious commission was running the official ferry service for the GB rowing team at the 2012 London Olympics.[3]

Modern Era

The firm re-entered the passenger boat market in 1980, at a time when the river was highly popular. The introduction of cheaper fibreglass craft enabled Hobbs to purchase one such vessel from Bounty Boats, the company it had already used for cabin cruisers. The single-deck 44-foot 6-inch fifty-seat river bus was named *Maratana*, after one of the famous Henley umpire launches. The decision was influenced by the success of Aquadine Enterprise Ltd of Wargrave that was often running its boats *Pink Champagne* (1975) and the larger Mississippi-style paddle steamer *Southern Comfort* (1979) in the Henley area. In 1981, the rival operator even applied to have a permanent restaurant mooring on Mill Meadows (the second such company to consider it).

Hobbs used *Maratana* for daily round trips (over the six-month season) along the regatta course with on-board commentary provided. The service was ideal for the era, as longer-distance cruises were falling out of fashion and passing through locks could cause considerable delays, which was why Salters cut its famous Oxford to Kingston run into shorter sections in 1974. By 1983, *Maratana* had carried around 20,000 people and its success led the firm to order another slightly longer craft (60 feet), *Consuta II*, from Bounty for £50,000.

Although the two river buses proved popular, they were not suitable for larger functions, which the firm often received enquiries about, especially in the run-up to major events. This led Hobbs to commission a £500,000 Mississippi-style stern paddle wheeler from Jakubait and Sons of Greenwich, which was introduced in 1991 and became the flagship of the fleet, as well as later the basis for the firm's current logo. The boat, which was designed by Don Tate Associates, was named *New Orleans* after Robert Fulton's famous Ohio craft of 1811. It was 115 feet long and weighed 75 tonnes, making it one of the largest of its kind on the non-tidal Thames with a licence for 175 passengers (although numbers were capped at 125 to ensure people's comfort). It offered a luxury panelled saloon, which could seat eighty people, as well as the latest safety standards, including an expensive sub-divided hull, which was one of the stipulations following the *Marchioness* disaster of 1989. Although the design raised some eyebrows for not being 'traditional', Tony Hobbs defended the decision by pointing out that paddle steamers were iconic craft that were recognised and reproduced around the world. Furthermore, there had been many on the Thames in the nineteenth century, albeit side-wheelers. It was officially launched in Henley by Sir Anthony Darrant MP, and the firm was soon offering Mississippi experiences with Cajun cooking and a resident jazz band on board. The vessel caused quite a stir when it arrived, as it was a dominant feature on the waterfront. Indeed, it was an unusually tall craft because of its two ornamental funnels that, like those on traditional Thames steamers, had to be lowered when passing through bridges. Forty-three residents petitioned the council against its mooring position in 1993, on the grounds of noise from customers and the view of the river being impaired. The complaint was dismissed, however, as councillor Tony Lane stressed that boats were 'part and parcel of Henley' and had always been there.[4] Indeed, the 'jewel in the crown' of the fleet came to be seen by many as an attractive feature of the waterfront and it proved particularly popular for private charters and corporate parties in the mid-1990s, as the country came of out of the recession. By 2016, *New Orleans* was estimated to have carried 300,000 passengers.

Further expansion came in 2001, when Hobbs commissioned another new boat, *Hibernia* – named after a different umpire launch – from Mustang Marine in Milford Haven. Delivering the 75-foot 5-inch craft was a considerable challenge, as it had to go by road to Penton Hook, which was one of the only locations the lorry could get to. Nicknamed the 'Dan Dare' boat, because of its unusual appearance, the £350,000 craft was intended to fill the size gap between the vessels, as it could be used for parties of up to sixty people. As a single-decked boat, it was also ideal for those with mobility difficulties. The addition also enabled the firm to dispense with *Maratana*, which was subsequently sold to Salters. A fourth large passenger was added in 2004, when *Waterman*, an 85-foot vessel that could carry parties of up to 100, was bought from Paul and Cheryl Bushnell of Wargrave.

The expansion of the fleet did not just increase the number of passengers the firm could carry at any one point, but, importantly, it also enabled Hobbs to extend the season, as the heated craft could be used all-year round. In 1984, for example, it encouraged local businesses to 'try something different this Christmas' by booking an office party on one of the craft. The festive cruises were one of many new and creative services that the company was also able to develop. Others included gin-tasting gatherings, wildlife cruises, afternoon

New Orleans
The 115-foot *New Orleans*, the £500,000 flagship of the fleet that was launched in 1991.
(© Sue Milton of www.thames-cards.co.uk)

Postcard, 1904
A 1904 postcard showing the waterfront north of the bridge and the three boat operators next to each other (Hobbs on the left, Hooper in the middle, and the Little White Hart Inn on the right).
(Author's collection)

teas, wedding charter packages and 'Midsomer Murder' events. The firm also offered children's entertainers, caricature artists and even a fireworks display by the bank, as well as a range of musical options, such as a DJ, swing and jazz duo, classically trained singers and an Elvis tribute band. These outsourced services also extended to decoration, professional lighting, photography and catering. One supplier of the latter was Charlotte Cavanagh, who won a local entrepreneur of the year award in 2017 for her 'Time for Tea' pop-up events.[5]

Collectively, the passenger boats were very important from a financial perspective, because they connected the firm with far greater numbers of customers and they could generate many additional forms of income, including drink purchases from the on-board bars. Furthermore, Hobbs endeavoured to keep the boats in a first-rate condition with a rigorous cleaning regime, as well as being discerning about what type of parties were accepted.

Competition

Despite the firm's current stature, its survival was far from assured in the early years, as there was a lot of competition on the river. Indeed, in 1896, during the 'golden age of the Thames', Emily Climenson recorded that Hobbs was one of *twelve* boat businesses in the town. Shepherd's enterprise at the Red Lion Hotel boathouse was by far the largest. It ran three launches from its prime location by the bridge (*Helen*, that could take fifty-nine passengers, and the smaller *Plover* and *Memoir*) and also offered skiffs, canoes, dinghies, fishing punts and sailing boats for hire. Hobbs received a much smaller write-up – albeit the second largest – and was commended for its 'fine range of boathouses filled with river craft of all descriptions', its accommodation for 200 boats, as well as its two steamers. The others mentioned were W. Parrott on Friday Street, Searle and Sons at the Royal Hotel (the famous Stangate business with a royal warrant), W. Clisby of the Little White Hart inn at Waterside (who could also recommend fishermen upon request), the Angel hotel (by the bridge on the Henley side, where fisherman could also be hired), the Carpenter's Arms boathouse (by the bridge on the Remenham side), James Harvey at Riverside (who was also a lessee of baths), and Thomas Smith of Riverside (who also offered a boat conveyance service of 1s per mile). In addition to these, there were large write-ups given to the specialist firms Kerbey Bowen and the Upper Thames Electric Launch Company, which both offered electric craft from near Marsh Lock, as well as Salters of Oxford. The latter was the dominant passenger boat operator on the non-tidal river with a monopoly on long-distance trips between Oxford and Kingston. It was therefore used by many travel firms, and a number of Henley hotels advertised in Thames guides to try to attract its passengers.

As the list suggests, the respective businesses were not all offering exactly the same services, but many of them were competing when it came to renting out small craft. As a result, it was not always peaceful existence between the competing operators. In 1988, John Hooper described how his ancestors had spoken of fights in the streets with boat hooks and paddles between the many boat-letters north of the bridge. That may have been an exaggeration, but it is not surprising that competition might have been quite cut-throat at times, as has been seen in the 'punt wars' in modern-day Cambridge.

By the end of the Edwardian period, the trade directories suggest that the field had thinned considerably, as there were only four major firms mentioned. In addition to Hobbs, these were Parrott, Searle and Salters. It was around that time that Hobbs dispensed with larger passenger boats, possibly because of the dominance of other businesses. Furthermore, there were other large operators nearby like Cawston's of Reading, which was running regular summer trips in Henley by the 1930s.

Although not mentioned in the trade directories, some of the waterside pubs of Henley would have continued to hire out boats. In 1918, a key acquisition for Hobbs was the

Red Lion Hotel, which came with a boathouse and river frontage. That was followed, in 1925, by the addition of Searle, a business without an heir to continue it, which resulted in Hobbs advertising that it was the successor of the famous enterprise. Indeed, acquiring competitors and property with water frontage were two of the main ways in which Hobbs grew its market share (see chapter 5).

By the mid-twentieth century the external competition had diminished, but the firm faced a new threat from *within* the family. The split began when Arthur purchased Meakes of Marlow in the 1930s. He was joined there by his second son, John, while his third, Allan, ended up working on the river in Moulsford. At that stage their side of the family posed no danger to the Hobbs in Henley, but during the Second World War, the oldest son, Cyril, bought the neighbouring business of Arlett and Sons, which was subsequently run under the Meakes banner. In his new place of employment, Cyril, who had worked at the Imperial Hotel and as a Section Officer Special Constable during the conflict, experienced a particularly harrowing episode. In 1947, he was unable to resuscitate a fifteen-year-old colleague, Derek Wheeler, who hanged himself in what appears to have been an April Fools' prank that went wrong.

By 1959, Cyril was operating under his own name from No. 11 Thames Side, the same year in which his boathouse was damaged when an unattended lorry rolled into it. Indeed, the road layout of Henley was such that vehicles ended up in the Thames from time to time. In 1987, five of Hobbs' staff successfully assisted in the rescue of a Mini that was left overhanging the river against a pile, after the owner had left the handbrake off. Similarly, in 1999, two wheels of an Audi, owned by customer John Barratt, went into the water by *New Orleans*. A more serious incident occurred in December 2001, when employee Mark Jones successfully went to the assistance of his friend, Alexandra Allen, who called him with freezing water up to her waste, after her car had slid on ice and plunged into the Thames by Riverside Terrace.

Cyril's rival operation produced considerable tension within the family, but it did not get as bad as in some other local firms. In 1931, for example, Henry Hooper failed in a legal action against his own brother, George, because the latter, who ran the riverside business, did not pay him anything from the jointly owned business that they had inherited from their father. Things were far worse in the Parrott family, however, after a feud broke out between the brothers Walter and Alfred. The former was accused of mistreating their mother, whom he lived with, and he even managed to abuse a judge, when the matter was brought before a court. A further incident occurred in 1927, when he came out of a pub and started an argument with his brother. A fight broke out that soon involved both sets of sons, including Alfred junior, who came to his father's aid and ended up throttling his uncle and threatening to kill him. Fortunately, the competition at Hobbs did not come to blows, and Cyril's enterprise was short-lived with him selling up to Maurice Parrott in the 1960s.

As the twentieth century drew on, manually powered vessels continued to fall out of favour and, as a result, many rental fleets on the river dwindled in size, leading to a number of operators folding. In Henley, some of the last remaining boat-letters made the transition to the less labour-intensive market of renting out mooring, which provided more consistent year-round income and did not require maintenance for boats or any storage space. Alf Parrott, who was building craft in the 1970s, made this switch in the 1980s, while John Hooper did so in the twenty-first century. The latter, who was a painter and decorator, still had twenty-six craft in 1988, including a number of traditional punts that were popular during the Henley Regatta. He described how the cut-throat competition of yesteryear had long since been replaced by a more cooperative approach. The 'rival' operators Tony Hobbs and Maurice Parrott had both helped him during his troubles around a decade earlier, when a dispute with Brakspear's led him to temporarily leave the trade.

This state of affairs was also partly a reflection of the relative strength of Hobbs. Even when Aquadine Enterprise of Wargrave appeared to be an increasing presence in the area in the late 1970s, the Henley firm introduced its own passenger boat service and soon grew the fleet to become the largest local operator. Indeed, by the twenty-first century, Hobbs reigned supreme when it came to most boating services in the local area, with the exception of some of those connected to the sport of rowing. Its pre-eminence extended to mooring too, as in 2019 it was responsible for 120 spaces of which seventy-five were owned by the firm. There was still inevitably some room in Henley for other boat companies to carve out revenue, especially when many craft congregated in the town during major events, but other local competition, including the once dominant Salters that maintained a limited presence in Henley, had well and truly been eclipsed.[6]

Marketing

Another ingredient of the success of Hobbs was its marketing. For much of its existence, the firm had a relatively conventional approach to promotion, consisting of attending boat shows and advertising in local newspapers and specialist publications. The former was not always successful, however, as in 1976, Hobbs was one of only a few companies involved with the disastrous Henley Boat Show, which only had nine craft on display and lost the organisers, Airfield Displays (Henley), around £15,000.

Hobbs was also able to rely on the visual marketing provided by certain showpiece craft, most notably the umpire launches that became associated with its fleet. Indeed, from the early 1920s onwards, the firm regularly advertised that it rented out the official Henley Royal Regatta craft. The association between Hobbs and these boats was reinforced in a number of newspaper articles, such as in 1992, when the *Daily Telegraph* reported that the company provided the 'launches used by the umpires at most of the famous regattas and races, including the Oxford and Cambridge Boat Race'. The firm's craft became even more conspicuous from the 1980s onwards with the addition of passenger boats. Indeed, the attractive and striking modern fleet stood out when moored up on the waterfront and the *New Orleans* was often used for photo shoots with the bridge providing a picturesque backdrop. In 1993, for example, the *Henley Standard* featured the Miss Henley contestants – a competition first held in 1979 – on board the craft. Furthermore, although there were some complaints about noise, the craft attracted even more attention when travelling up and down the waterway, especially when the parties had musical accompaniment.

Re-entering the passenger boat market in the 1980s also enabled the firm to introduce new and creative forms of marketing, such as running competitions, offering prizes for organisations (in the form of river trips) and sometimes giving complimentary boats for fundraising events. The latter included cruises for Henley Football Club in 2016, a team many of the Hobbs family had played for, and the Gurkha Welfare Trust in 2017, the fighting force after which the firm's first passenger boat was named. These many initiatives were in keeping with the family's commitment to the civic affairs of Henley (see chapter 6), but were also good marketing opportunities. Indeed, many of them captured the spirit of the age, such as in 2019, when Hobbs offered a free rowing boat for anyone wanting to clear up rubbish from the waterway.

The firm did not just assist other organisations with fundraising, but, from the late twentieth century onwards, a notable feature of its marketing strategy was cooperating with like-minded local agencies to produce mutually beneficial results. Jonathan Hobbs was the chairman of Visit Thames and the Thames Boating Trades Association, as well as being heavily involved in many Henley initiatives and events. The company also helped to organise some river events, like the Henley and Wargrave Boat Show.

Suzy Hobbs played an important role in managing the business relationships and developing the overall brand, which included introducing an in-house gin (see chapter 6). Her work was recognised in 2019, when she was one of thirty nominees (across three counties) for the Sue Ryder Women of Achievement Award.

One key area she focused on was developing the firm's digital marketing, including the all-important website. In 2012, Google described Henley as a 'digital trailblazer' with Hobbs being one of the businesses that was said to have embraced the new technology. Indeed, in 2016, the firm introduced online booking, making it easy for customers to rent out craft, and ensuring that the company received the payment in advance. This was an important development, because previously those who booked over the phone did not always turn up. It was also the same year in which the firm was awarded a prize from TripAdvisor, as one of the top holiday lettings companies in the country. Hobbs' services also featured in the *Daily Mail*'s *Event* magazine in 2017, as one of the 'six of the best British boating trips for all the family'.

Furthermore, the business also benefited from being used in television and film work, such as when its boats were used in the making of *The Theory of Everything*, the movie about Stephen Hawking (released in 2014). Other productions included Eamonn Holmes and Ruth Langsford being transported at the Henley Royal Regatta as part of the *A Taste of the High Life* series for Channel 5 in 2015, and Jonathan Hobbs taking Michael Portillo on a slipper launch for his BBC2 show *Great British Railway Journeys* in 2019.

A more novel public display came in March 2018 when a Hobbs boat was used by artist Clive Hemsley when he attached 800 white LED lights to Henley Bridge. Over 2,000 people signed a petition to retain the attractive feature, but as it did not have official sanction the installation had to be removed. The following year, after many of the major bridges of London had been lit in a multi-million pound 'Illuminated River' project, Hemsley applied for planning permission to reinstate his creation.[7]

Final Thoughts

Each year thousands of customers enjoy cruises on board the passenger boats of Hobbs, in what is the most visible aspect of the firm's activities. Indeed, a trip on the river is considered a 'must-do' activity for many visitors to the regatta town. The craft have hosted all kinds of parties, including a talk by journalist Matthew Engel in 2015, and the launch of Professor Anne Jones' book *The Educational Roundabout* the following year. Other notable clients included model Liz Hurley, whose party was unfortunately immobilised by flood conditions; actor Russell Brand, who had his wedding reception afloat; singer Barbara Streisand, who was taken on a trip on *Enchantress*; and the Ball family, who enjoyed an outing with the music provided by Zoe Ball's husband, Norman Cook (DJ Fatboy Slim).

Although the private charter market could be lucrative, it was still vulnerable to changes in the economy. That is one reason why some of the firm's other less noticeable activities were important for maintaining a regular cash flow and helping Hobbs to out-compete some of its competitors. Perhaps the most important of these was the development of the company's property portfolio.

Chapter 5

Property

The Victorian and Edwardian periods ... saw Henley's final transformation into a fashionable social resort, known across the world for its annual Regatta, and boasting an eclectic range of impressive new buildings to match its new-found prestige.

Simon Townley[1]

By the start of the twentieth century, Hobbs was neither one of the largest nor best-known firms on the river, but by using loans, mortgages and debentures, it steadily built up a property empire both in Henley and in nearby riverside locations. There were three main reasons for the purchase of the different sites: diversifying and growing the market share, keeping competitors out, and providing jobs for the family.

Expansion: Diversifying and Growing the Market Share

In order to grow, the firm initially acquired more land in the close vicinity of the Ship with new boathouses built *c*. 1884 and in 1887. After the pub closed in 1897, the family pursued further expansion on the south side of the bridge with the purchase of property on Station Road in 1898 (where the new headquarters was built for £228 11*s* 5*d*) and Mill Meadows in 1902 (£3,250). Indeed, in 1904, the *Henley and South Oxfordshire Standard* claimed that the firm had doubled in size in just over a decade.

Hobbs' initial location near the regatta's course finish line may have provided a good vantage point for watching the races, but despite claiming in advertising that it was five minutes from the station, there were many other Thames businesses better placed to gain trade from those arriving by train. Indeed, that was one reason why the firm added a site on Station Road, as it was in a superior position to pick up the casual customers arriving by the railway. The latter was also close to the riverside promenade at Mill Meadows, which many visitors flocked to. Bill Hobbs had been the key figure in acquiring the site for the council, which in 1930 boasted an extensive pleasure ground with a garden, play area, green (comprising tennis courts, putting and bowling greens) and an ornamental lake. The firm's expansion in Henley continued with the main additions being the Red Lion Hotel and boathouse in 1917, which came with the Wargrave Road yard; Searle and Sons in 1925 (for £2,000), which included the Central Garage; and Thamesfield in 1937 (for £1,200).

In 1907, Hobbs entered a new phase of expansion by adding land outside of the town with the acquisition of East's yard in Shiplake (for £3,500), which was followed a year later by that of Ellis in Goring (£3,000). In 1911, the firm bought the capacious Springfield works of

Sam Saunders near Goring, which enabled it to build large steel craft. The site cost £250 for the leasehold, which was followed by a second payment of £500 in 1912 for the freehold. Further property in Shiplake was added in 1912 (two plots) and 1941 (Cordery's boathouse for £2,000), and in Pangbourne in 1932 (Franklin's yard) and 1940 (Ashley's boathouse for £2,450).

These sites opened up new rental markets, as well as allowing the firm to offer a greater variety of facilities. The yard in Goring, for example, had a covered dock that could accommodate six 50-foot launches (without the need of hauling the craft out) and by 1925, the firm owned four slipways (three at Henley and one at Goring). The additions also enabled Hobbs to offer a vast amount of storage, which was an important source of income outside the summer season. When the company owned the sites in Henley, Shiplake and Goring, it was able to advertise that it could accommodate 800 small boats and 100 launches, but after the Pangbourne properties were acquired, it claimed that it could store an incredible 1,000 boats and 150 launches. The figures are suspiciously round and high, but Hobbs was undoubtedly one of the largest providers of pleasure boat storage on the river at that time. The sites were also used for different activities over the years and one substantial change was the conversion of the boatbuilding yard on Station Road into a chandlery in 1965.

The programme of expansion was not a complete success, however, as some of the opportunities fell through. In 1907, the firm offered £7,000 for Meakes and Redknap of Marlow, but the sale did not happen, although Arthur subsequently acquired the business in the 1930s. In 1925, the firm pulled out of an agreement to buy another site in Shiplake that not only included a boathouse, garage, tennis courts and a motor garage, but would have given Hobbs the monopoly of the village's water frontage. A price of £4,250 was agreed, but after two of the craft that were supposed to be in the sale were spotted in the possession of a neighbouring Henley boat-letter (Harvey's), the firm walked away from the deal on principle. The following year, Hobbs also had the opportunity to buy the Firs Boathouse off New Street (owned by Fawley Court) for £2,700, but decided against it, only to then purchase it two decades later for £3,550.[2]

Expansion: Keeping Competitors Out

Appropriating the property of competitors helped the firm increase its market share by providing more facilities and locations to operate from – and a greater visibility in an area. In the highly territorial world of boat-letting, it also reduced the already limited amount of water frontage that was available to others. Indeed, that was a key part of Hobbs' business model, as it targeted sites that came with riverside mooring that could be retained, even if the main property was sold. The purchase of Thamesfield in 1937 was a prime example of this 'asset stripping', as the twenty-one-bedroom house on 9 acres of land also came with a quarter of a mile of mooring space. The firm retained some of the water frontage, while selling the house, which was subsequently used by the Thamesfield Youth Association, before being turned into a nursing home.

Hobbs owned a large amount of mooring by that point, as it had acquired the Red Lion Hotel on the eve of the First World War, which had 250 feet of water frontage, while it also had 400 feet by Station Road and another 150 feet near the original boathouse overlooking the regatta course. Although the family's interest in the hotel ended in 1937 (see below), the streamside section of the island opposite Station Road was gained six years later (for £150), in order to prevent opposition coming in. Furthermore, importantly, the firm also increased the 'surface area' of the existing water frontage by building finger jetties in the 1960s to enable greater numbers of craft to moor up. As the river was becoming increasing popular at that time, there was greater demand for facilities and, in the mid-1970s, the town council sought to ban permanent moorings at some of its sites, in order to maintain the appearance of the waterside.

Indeed, the limited amount of space meant that there were inevitably occasional disputes over access to property, especially at busy periods. In 2014, for example, Hobbs paid the council to have exclusive use of the frontage by the Red Lion until 31 July, but this led to objections from four companies that had shared it the previous year, even though they had refused to pay the increased fee. Despite the opposition, the firm is still leasing the mooring today.[3]

Expansion: Providing Jobs for the Family

Although the expansion outside of Henley could be seen as a financial decision to forge new markets for the firm, it was strongly influenced by the more pragmatic need to provide work for the five brothers. In order to give two of them more meaningful jobs – and presumably more space for all of them – Frederick was assigned to Goring and Ernest to Shiplake, while Arthur later chose to run Meakes in Marlow. Ultimately, that was not enough to keep everyone happy though, as inevitably some family members embraced other careers (see chapter 6).

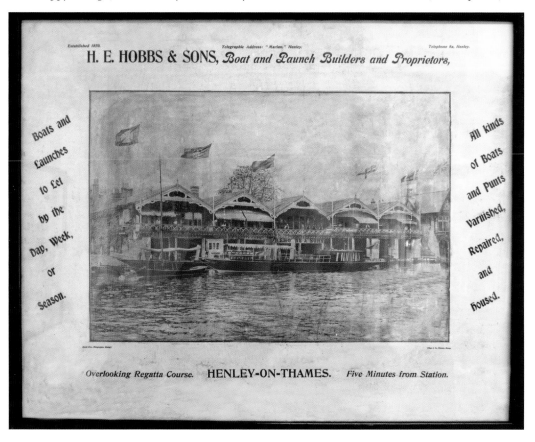

Advertisement for H. E. Hobbs and Sons, *c.* 1900
A framed advert (*c.* 1900) showing the Wharfe Lane Boathouses (built in 1887) with two steamers and a sailing boat moored outside. (© Hobbs of Henley)

Building the Station Road Site, 1898
The Station Road property being built in 1898 at a cost of £228 11s 5d. (© Hobbs of Henley)

New Areas for the Business

The firm's expansion also opened up the potential for other forms of property development. Hobbs pulled down the old granaries and cottages at the end of New Street – considered to be an eyesore by many – and built in their place a number of attractive boathouses with verandas. Completed in 1887 and known collectively as the Wharfe Lane Boathouses, they were a prime location from which to watch the regatta and one guidebook described them as 'one of the most striking features of the river-side at Henley'. They also had accommodation above them that could be rented out or used by staff, which was presumably why a flat was also built above the Red Lion Boathouse in 1923.

One unusual departure for Hobbs was the acquisition of Higgs and Company in 1897, the printing and bookbinding firm at Caxton House on Station Road. Harry, William and Albert bought the business from Thomas Higgs' widow, in partnership with another investor, Charles Luker. The printing firm, which was said to be in a perilous state at the time, produced the *Henley and South Oxfordshire Standard* newspaper (now the *Henley Standard*) and the official Henley Royal Regatta programme. The previous Foreman, R. W. Jacobs, was retained, but in 1900, the Hobbs brothers agreed to sell their stake in the company to their business partner. That was not the family's last interaction with Luker, as Bill later worked with him on the town council. He became one of the most distinguished public servants of his generation and, as well as being mayor numerous times, he was given the rare honour of being made a Freeman of the town.

Not all of their development plans were accepted, however. In 1962, a major project put forward by a consortium that included Dick Hobbs and the trustees of Bill's estate was rejected. The idea was to convert the Central and Rolfe's Garages into a block of ten-storey flats, but the proposal was branded a 'shocker' in a town council meeting, as the buildings were to be 135 feet tall and would have dwarfed even St Mary's church tower. Indeed, one councillor commented that the structure would not have been suitable for Reading, let alone Henley.

By the following decade, many of the firm's yards were no longer needed and they were therefore developed, rented out or sold (see below). Hobbs converted some of the property in Goring to flats, with one site taken over by a dental surgery in 1984. Indeed, at the end of the twentieth century waterside buildings became particularly valuable, as new development on the Thames was discouraged and property prices in the area rose sharply. The need to manage the assets more tax efficiently (in relation to VAT) was recognised in 2005, when the parent company was demerged into Hobbs of Henley Ltd – a name the firm was already using informally for the boating side of the business – and Millpool Properties Ltd. By 2015, the latter, which managed the property in Goring, had become more like 'Hobbs and Daughters' than 'Hobbs and Sons', as the shareholders were largely female members of the family. Jackie and Jonathan each held a quarter of the shares, Melanie and Katherine (Jonathan's sisters) both had 16.3 per cent each, Tony had 10 per cent, while Pamela Drury (Cassie Hobbs' granddaughter) and Wendy Pytches (the sister of Eddie Hobbs' widow) had 4.1 per cent and 3.2 per cent respectively. By that stage, a further notable development that had occurred to the property retained by the boat side of the business was the conversion of the chandlery into a restaurant, which provided a consistent year-round income. Despite some objections from nearby residents, La Barca restaurant opened in 2011, which became Shaun Dickens at the Boatyard two years later.[4]

Sales

The property portfolio was important because parts of it could be offloaded when money was needed or if someone made an attractive offer. Many of the transactions were relatively small, such as the sales of Wharf Cottage in 1911 (to Miss Lather for £400), land by Goring Lock in 1922 (to the Thames Conservancy for £400), and part of the island opposite Station Road in 1944 (to Colonel Millard for £200, on condition of him not conducting any commercial activity from the site). Yet there were also some more substantial deals, such as the sale of 'Madura' in Shiplake in 1934 for £2,850, the nearby Bolney Boathouse and Bungalow in 1947 for £2,750, and the Springfield yard in 1949 for £2,275. The latter, which subsequently became part of Withymead Nature Reserve, was partly to fund the building of a wet dock at the Wargrave Road yard. By 1954, the firm owned five slipways, three of which were in Henley and two of which were in Pangbourne. The sites at the latter were sold after good offers were received for them and in 1975, property in Shiplake, which had been refurbished for residential use, was sold for £32,500, partly in order to pay Dick's death duties. Furthermore, in 1986, Hobbs financed the modernisation of the Station Road and Wargrave Road properties by selling land next to the former. Ironcliffe Estates built eleven four-bedroom houses and eight 2-bedroom flats on the 1½-acre site. A first-floor office was added on Station Road at the time and a permanent kiosk was also established on the site of where there had been a temporary one. The firm leased the latter to a company selling ice creams and other refreshments, as well as sub-letting to it another kiosk closer to the Angel (once used by Arlett), partly in order to prevent other boat operators using it.[5] The land owned by Hobbs is now largely confined to Henley with the exception of the four properties at the Goring boathouse, managed by Millpool.

Flood Levels
The ever-present threat of flooding shown by the water level markers on the side of the Hobbs'
office in Station Road in 2019. (© Simon Wenham)

Fire at the Wargrave Road yard, 2004
The devastating fire that ripped through the Wargrave Road boatyard on 5 August 2004.
(© Reproduced by permission of the *Henley Standard* from 6 August 2004)

Challenges

Owning property could be lucrative, but it also posed some challenges. One was simply the upkeep of sites, which could be large at times, such as in 1958, when the firm's profits were dented by work that had to be carried out on a large storage shed on Wargrave Road, coupled with repairs to *Magician*.

One of the most persistent threats was flooding. The area around Mill Meadows was particularly susceptible and, in 1903, the firm had to postpone the construction of a house by it because of the issue. The river tended to be slightly higher in the winter and spring months anyway, but occasionally extremes of weather caused buildings to be inundated. The highest water levels are still marked on the side of the firm's offices.

Although there was much less revenue generated in the colder months, the freezing winter of 1890/1 was so extreme that fishermen and watermen were said to have made money fitting skates for those who wanted to go on the ice, while Tom Shepherd of the Red Lion gave river trips on a modified sailing sledge. It is not clear whether Hobbs was able to cash in on the freeze, although some festivities occurred close to its yard, such as a bonfire being lit *on the river* opposite it.

There were also a number of fires that affected the firm's properties. In 1908, the employees of Hobbs helped to tackle a 'very serious' blaze at Messrs J. Putman and Sons, a rope, tent and tarpaulin manufacturer on Friday Street. The Anchor pub was narrowly saved and a piece of burning canvas landed on Hobbs' boathouse, but was fortunately spotted before it caused any more damage. Similarly, in 1949, a combustion stove overheated and caused a roof fire at the boat company, but it was discovered early enough and extinguished. The firm was not so lucky in 2004, however, when considerable damage was done to the Wargrave Road site. Fifty firefighters battled to quell the 100-foot flames, which caused thousands of pounds of damage to boat-repairing equipment and a camping exhibition.

Another problem with riverside property was that it was prone to vandalism. Sometimes this was the result of specific events, like the election of 1906, which caused 'a few of the more enthusiastic spirits on either side' to vent their feelings by defacing the posters and bills of their opponents. The *Henley and South Oxfordshire Standard* reported that 'some damage was done at Messrs. Hobbs and Sons' boathouses and a reward was offered for information which lead to the conviction of the offender.' The issue became more acute in the second half of the century. In 1974, the firm opposed the idea of holding a 'Pops on the Prom' music festival during the regatta week on the grounds that damage might be done to craft, as had occurred at the Reading Festival. Hobbs experienced an unusual act of vandalism in October 1979, when workforce arrived one morning to find many of the company's boats drifting down the river. A seventeen-year-old youth was found to be responsible, who had untied the craft after consuming at least ten pints. The firm also sometimes helped in the aftermath of vandalism that affected others; in November 2017, it retrieved items from the river, after a group had thrown the statue of a mermaid and some umbrellas into it from the lawn of the Red Lion.

A further problem sometimes connected with vandalism was theft. One particularly large robbery occurred in May 1977, when Richard Woodcroft from South Africa had £2,000 of currency taken from *Girl Katherine* while it was moored up at Hobbs. In the summer of 2006, there was a 'crime wave' on the river stretching from Henley to Wargrave, which affected a number of boats, including ten at Hobbs' Thamesfield mooring. 2016 was another bad year as Director Peter Herbert had a motor home stolen from a yard in April, while fifteen craft were targeted in November with an estimated £15,000 worth of outboard motors taken.

A more unusual crime occurred at the firm's moorings in 1953, when Leonard Beckett successfully brought an action against Reginald Perry, after one of the latter's dogs bit him on the leg when he was delivering coke to a neighbouring launch. The owner showed little remorse and not only claimed that if he had been the animal, he would also have taken exception to someone dressed like Beckett, but also that the Hobbs family had said that the property was not a public right of way anyway.

Little did he know that access to the riverside would become one of the town's most protracted political disputes. The subject was raised by a Thames River Walk Committee that sought to open up the towpath for walkers, as well as the National Parks and Access to Countryside Act of 1949, which required county councils to produce maps showing the location of any bridle paths and footpaths. The matter came to a head in 1956, the same year in which the town's first female mayor was elected, parking charges were introduced in Mill Meadows, and mysterious footprints (that turned out to be a hoax by students) were discovered outside the Little White Hart Hotel that were dubbed 'the abominable river man'. Tony Hobbs argued that the section of the river between Station Road and the promenade was not a public footpath, but was instead part of the towpath for which access was granted through licence from the Thames Conservancy. As the firm had built a slipway and cutting on the site, it wanted to retain the right to close the footpath off, when the bridge needed to be opened to let boats in or out (the equivalent of around five weeks every year). A legal agreement from Drewett and Cooper in 1898 was produced, as well as one with the Thames Conservancy from 1926, showing that the firm paid 4s 2d to lease the land. The company reassured the public that it did not want to keep anyone away, but was simply exercising its legal right to shut the path, which it maintained by closing the walkway one day per year, a practice it had done since 1907. Many townsfolk spoke out on the matter, before Oxford County Council initially ruled in Hobbs' favour, before changing its decision on the basis that the path had not been closed prior to 1907.

That was not the end of the matter, however, as the town council continued to discuss the matter of establishing a walkway by the Thames. It initially focused on the section north of the bridge, but disputes over the ownership of land by the Little White Hart and Riverside Terrace led to the whole affair being delayed until 1988 and, even then, it was not until bollards were placed in 1991 that the path was usable. The fate of the walkway south of the river continued to be discussed into the twenty-first century.[6]

Drink

Given that the business started in a pub, it is not surprising that Hobbs had lingering connections with the drinks industry. Indeed, pleasure boating and the consumption of alcohol were often thought to be connected, which led to some concern. In 1906, for example, parliament discussed the problem of 'floating beerhouses' (passenger boats) that were operating on the river.

The received wisdom from within the family was that Harry Hobbs was quite a character, who was particularly fond of his home-brewed gin. A court case in 1875 confirms his affinity to the drink, as he was charged with serving it on the premises half an hour earlier (at 5.30 p.m.) than was permitted by law on a Sunday. He was caught out in rather comical circumstances. A policeman who heard voices in the pub went in to investigate and was greeted by an explosion on the fire, suggesting that someone had quickly thrown a drink on it. The men inside the room protested their innocence by claiming that they were simply having tea, but their cause was not helped by the fact that one of Harry's sons was clearly hiding something behind his back. When questioned, he rather unconvincingly said that he was not holding anything and raised one empty hand as proof. Upon being asked to show what he had in the other, he reluctantly revealed a quarter measure, which upon inspection was found to have had gin in it. Despite the appearance of guilt, Harry successfully claimed that the friend often brought his grandchildren to play with his children, and that he had given him the drink, but had not sold it.

Nor was this his only brush with the law. The Ship, which was a substantial domestic house with a warehouse and a carpenter's shop, was situated by a major wharf that was the only local landing place with a campshot and crane. As a result, it was frequented by commercial river workers and this occasionally led to trouble, such as in 1888, when a 'rumpus' broke out between four bargemen. The men had started a sparring match for fun, which then escalated into a full-on fight. After being asked to leave, one of them, James Wilkins, who was visiting his brother-in-law who had arrived by tugboat, became quarrelsome and struck Harry in the eye, knocking him and one his children down in the process. The police were sought and Wilkins continued to be aggressive, while using 'some very bad expressions'. He later apologised in court, but was given a fine, despite his protestations that he had never been worse for drink in his life and that it was actually Harry who had given *him* a black eye.

Harry was not just a publican, however. By 1890, he had become the vice chairman of the Henley and District Beer, Wine and Spirit Protection Society. The organisation, which was headed up by Archibald Brakspear, was formed in 1885 to look after the interests of the trade. Harry also regularly attended events of the Licensed Victuallers until 1897, when the Ship closed.

That was not the end of the family's association with public houses, however. In 1917, Bill and Arthur bought the famous Red Lion Hotel (and rented the lawn in front of it). The notable coaching house was not only the headquarters of Henley Rowing Club, but it had welcomed many illustrious guests throughout its long history, including George III, Charles I, George IV, Grace Kelly and Winston Churchill, as well as Shenstone, who was said to have etched his famous poem about inns on one of its window panes. In 1919, Arthur, who ran the establishment, had the embarrassment of being hauled before the courts on a charge of serving beer above the maximum price (by 6*d*), at a time when his brother, Bill (the co-owner), was not only a magistrate, but the Mayor of Henley. The problem was that higher prices were changed in the 'more select' lounge, which led to an action being brought by disgruntled customers, even though their food bills had been reduced on complaint. The manageress, Miss Hill, who received a fine, took full responsibility for the indiscretion and admitted that she was not aware of the law. A more unusual court case occurred in 1935, when Frank Rebbitt, the pub's head waiter, was charged with attempted theft. Fortunately for him he was acquitted after it became apparent that, in an inebriated state, he had decided to climb the roof, only to then open the office window and fall into it, possibly mistaking it for a door.

The Red Lion regularly applied for late licences for special events and, in 1929, there was an insight into how busy it normally was. The Licensed Victuallers Protection Association appealed to the borough's authorities to move the Sunday licensing hours forward by half an hour (from the usual time of 12.30 p.m. to 2.30 p.m.), but Arthur Hobbs was one of the few against it. He claimed many of his customers came from outside of the town and therefore a later meal time was preferable to them. He suggested that between April and September the establishment had served 1,400 luncheons. Moreover, he added that 15 per cent of his customers used to come by car, but it was now as high as 88 per cent. The increasing number of people arriving in this manner is precisely the reason why the boat firm was offering free parking by the mid-1930s for those renting out craft (except during the Henley Regatta), as space for cars was an increasingly valuable commodity in the town.

Arthur's observation also gives an insight into how changing modes of transportation were affecting businesses in Henley, as it was a place where many vehicles converged in order to cross the Thames or visit the resort. Although the town was not a manufacturing centre for the motor industry – with the exception of a few Stuart Stellar motorcycles and Squire Cars that were produced in the 1910s and 1930s respectively – this 'first era of mass

Norwegian Rowers
Norwegian rowers in the 1920s with Hobbs' Red Lion Hotel and yard in the background, where three motor boats (including two umpire launches) can be seen moored. (© River and Rowing Museum, Henley-on-Thames)

Mr Hobbs Gin
Two flavoured gins (rhubarb and ginger, and raspberry and elderflower) that were introduced to the Mr Hobbs range in 2019. (© Mr Hobbs gin)

motoring' caused it considerable problems. Not only did road accidents become increasingly common – forcing magistrates like Bill and Dick to commit more time to dealing with them (see chapter 6) – but the traffic and parking problems got so bad that they were soon regarded as almost insurmountable challenges. The council repeatedly introduced new measures to try to deal with the issues, such as parking restrictions, speed limits, different one-way systems and traffic lights. There were many other suggested solutions that were never carried out, like demolishing the Angel, building another bridge, and even constructing a tunnel under the river.

Although the family's association with running public houses ended before the Second World War, the firm had a licensed restaurant on its property again in 2011. Furthermore, the reintroduction of passenger boat services in the 1980s rekindled its connection with the hospitality industry and led to a whole range of catering options being offered to clients (see chapter 4).

In 2017, one new venture associated with this was the launch of Mr Hobbs gin, in conjunction with the Foxdenton distillery, based in Buckinghamshire. The initiative, which was the brainchild of Suzy Hobbs, further enhanced the company's brand. Indeed, the creative marketing harked back to the history of the firm by focussing on the character of Harry Hobbs and the supposed re-creation of his recipe, while linking the business to a fashionable product. The drink was used in new advertising initiatives, such as promoting a gin trail in conjunction with Brakspear and ten pubs in 2018, and sponsoring Rewind Festival in 2019. The latter was when the firm's range was expanded further with the introduction of two new fruit-flavoured gin liqueurs (rhubarb and ginger, and raspberry and elderflower).[7]

Final Thoughts

In 2013, Tony Hobbs, the owner of one historic boat business, hosted a ceremony to recognise the heritage of another, Sam Saunders of Goring, when an Oxfordshire Blue Plaque was placed on the premises. His own company had played an important role in shaping the physical appearance of the waterfront at Henley. Unsurprisingly, many famous people used its sites, including members of the royal family who attended the regatta, such as George V and Queen Mary in 1912, and Princess Anne in 1977. Many performers had connections with the business too, such as Jimmy Page and Robert Plant, who rented a property in Pangbourne (Ashley's boathouse); Max Miller, the 'cheekie chappy' comedian, who stayed in a caravan in the Wargrave Road yard site when performing in the area; Vince Hill, who regularly travelled to the waterfront; and the group Madness, who posed in a boat by the bridge in 1986, as part of Mike Read's Radio 1 breakfast show. The company's Shiplake site was used in a BBC thriller *The Girl in the Black Bikini* in 1966, while the Rotary Club's first annual 'rowlock rally' finished at the Hobbs yard in 1971.[8]

Ultimately, the firm's expansion provided Hobbs with an extensive asset base that could be leveraged in many different ways. It was also important for establishing its territorial dominance, as well as opening up more consistent year-round sources of income. Nevertheless, the success of the business cannot be measured by its assets alone, as it is also important to acknowledge the crucial role that different family members played in building up the enterprise.

Chapter 6

Family

...the Hobbs family is noted for its public service getting on for seventy uninterrupted years, in fact, it is equally well-known for the boating business it runs.

Henley Standard, 1979[1]

A history of Hobbs would be incomplete without describing the family behind the business. In 1891, there were only two individuals involved, as Kelly's trade directory listed the firm as 'Henry Edward Hobbs and Son' (Bill), rather than 'Sons'. When Harry, the founder, died on New Year's Day in 1910, having suffered from a series of strokes, the local newspaper did not accord him any great importance. Nevertheless, one effect of his passing was that his former home of Belmont House (No. 23 New Street), close to where a number of the family lived in the early years of the business, was given to the Board of Guardians to care for twelve children.

By that stage they were not even the best-known Hobbs family in Henley. That distinction went to the prominent builder Benjamin Hobbs and his architect son, A. Edward (see chapter 1). Indeed, the surname was shared by many others in the area, which meant that, from time to time, the firm had to publicly distance itself from certain individuals. In 1897, for example, the *Henley and South Oxfordshire Standard* had to be notified after a different Arthur Hobbs was convicted of shooting a pheasant in Marlow, as also occurred in 1905, when the newspaper wrongly stated that a Hobbs was involved in a slander case.[2]

W. A. Hobbs (Bill)

It was Harry's second son, Bill, who was credited by the family with building up the business. As one town councillor put it in 1904, he was 'intimately concerned with the steady rise of the firm'. In 1913, another said he was the kind of person who was bound to get to the top of whatever position in life he found himself in, given his energy, diligence and industriousness. Indeed, Bill, who was born six years earlier than his next brother, Arthur, was a remarkable individual whose upward trajectory can be traced by the various roles he held.[3]

Fire Brigade

Bill's public service began in 1883, when he became involved in the twelve-strong voluntary fire brigade. By 1885, he had risen to the rank of Pioneer and, in 1891, he was made its Superintendent (and later its Treasurer). As one of its most active and capable servants, he was often the first on the scene of a fire (day or night) and was honoured a number of times for his long service; in 1908 he received a twenty-five-year service medal. The brigade dealt with many residential fires in the town centre, as well as damage to larger properties, such as Harpsden Court in 1897 and the Congregational Church in 1907. A report in 1910 stated that during the previous year, the brigade had conducted twenty drills and had had seven call-outs.

His role also required him to attend all kinds of civic functions and in 1910 he was one of two Henley representatives from the fire brigade to be in the Guard of Honour at the Royal Funeral for King Edward VII. He retired from the service two years later, probably because of his advancing age, coupled with his increasing commitments elsewhere (see below).[4]

Military Service

As well as being part of the fire brigade, Bill joined the 2nd Volunteer Oxfordshire Light Infantry (D company), which also participated in major civic events, including the laying of the foundations of the new Town Hall in 1899. By that point, he had been made a Sergeant and was serving alongside Private F. Hobbs (presumably his brother, Frederick). Bill, who was also a member of the Henley Rifle Club, won the Old Bolney Cup for the best aggregate shot for close firing at the annual Volunteer's prize meeting in 1900, and by 1908, he had risen to the rank of Quarter-Master-Sergeant.

Getting enough recruits was a constant challenge, as many local employers did not allow their men time off to attend the drills. Nevertheless, numerous appeals managed to get the numbers at the Territorial Army (as it had been renamed) up to between sixty and seventy men from the Henley area by the time the First World War broke out.

Although he was not required to serve, as he was in his fifties – not to mention being the Mayor of Henley at the time (see below) – Bill opted to fight with his fellow soldiers. He served in France for a year and ten months, during which his winery in Henley was robbed. In November 1916, he was part of a battalion that embarked upon a gruelling 70-mile trek from Robecq to Neuvillette (in the Somme). The journey took a great toll on the men's shoes and although he personally went to great lengths to procure mending leather for them, he was unsuccessful. He was promoted to Captain during his service and returned to Henley after bidding a 'reluctant farewell' to his men.

Serving abroad also meant that he missed the wedding of Cassie, his oldest daughter, to Louis Drury. The event occurred in September 1914 – the same month in which another Henley councillor, J. T. Campion, achieved the notable distinction of being detained on suspicion of spying while on holiday in Bognor Regis. At the time, it was not uncommon for wedding gifts to be published in the *Henley and South Oxfordshire Standard*, in a rather unforgiving public record of someone's generosity (or lack of it). In this instance, the bridegroom kindly gave his wife a cheque, receiving a lounge chair in return. The other presents included a baby grand piano (and cheque) from Bill, a silver tea service from Reginald, and an assortment of eclectic items, including a crumb brush, doily, dinner gong, oil painting, silver ink stand and, the *pièce de résistance*, a 'handsome silver egg stand and silver sardine fork' from the Young Helpers League, an organisation Cassie helped out with. She and other family members were also very active in many of the local fundraising initiatives to support the troops.

As the conflict dragged on and the death toll mounted – much of which was reported in the local newspaper – many individuals sought special exemption from military service. In the summer of 1917, one of them was Ernest Hobbs, aged forty-one, who gave the excuse that he had the boats of eighty customers to look after, beside those of the firm's. Arthur also spoke on his behalf and pointed out that Bill was already in active service, while Frederick had been sent from their Goring yard to stores at Didcot. The exemption for Ernest was refused, but an allowance was made that he could not be called up until after 30 September. His youngest brother, Albert, who had served with Bill in the fire brigade, was sent to Mesopotamia, where he was fittingly attached to the water transport section of the Royal Engineers. Some of the next generation were also old enough to fight, including Bill's son, Dick, who served for eighteen months with the 28th London Regiment, gaining his Physical Therapy instructor's certificate in the process.

Bill returned to Henley and served on the County Bench, before being elected mayor again, in time for the Armistice. After the conflict, he became the key individual involved in the creation of the War Memorial Hospital, the town's tribute to those who had died. This was seen as being particularly fitting given that Bill was its 'victory mayor', who had himself worn the King's uniform.

An interesting postscript to the story is that his oldest son did not share his father's unwavering commitment to the military. After becoming an accountant, Reginald travelled to Jamaica and, although he joined the volunteers and became a Colour Sergeant, in 1915, he was charged with unlawfully absenting himself from the parades, despite having written to resign from his post. In what was described in the *Kingston Daily Gleaner* as a 'very interesting case', he was eventually acquitted, only to then pass away three months later of typhoid, at the age of only twenty-three.[5]

Fire Brigade
The volunteer fire brigade in the 1890s, when Bill Hobbs was Superintendent. (Courtesy of Henley Fire Brigade)

The 2/4th Oxfordshire and Buckinghamshire Light Infantry, 1914
Members of the 2/4th Oxfordshire and Buckinghamshire Light Infantry at New College, Oxford, in 1914. Bill Hobbs may be the man to the left (as you look at the photo) of the officer holding the walking stick. (© Reproduced by permission of the *Henley Standard* from 22 August 1914)

Political Service

Bill's civic duties for the fire brigade and volunteer army may have been a stepping stone to his political career, but he cut his political teeth in the 1890s, as a member of the (Conservative) Salisbury Club. It was not until 1904, however, that he was nominated by the Town Clerk (and firm's solicitor), John Cooper, to fill a vacant town council seat. His appointment was unopposed and he went on to enjoy a long and distinguished career, which included serving on the county council from 1907. He was a staunch Conservative whose 'business-like ability', diligent attention and 'consistent, genuine and honest work' saw him rise up the political ranks. He gained the respect and confidence of his colleagues for fearlessly sticking to his principles, as someone who was as 'straight as a gun-barrel', but with 'no axe to grind'.

Fate conspired against him, however, after he was unanimously voted as the mayor-elect in 1911, only to then lose his seat in the election, before he could take up the post. He was then re-elected the following year and although he became mayor in 1913, he was not able to serve a full term, after he relinquished his post in order to fight in the First World War.

After returning to Henley, he made up for lost time by serving an unprecedented four consecutive years as mayor, from 1918 onwards. Indeed, he seemed quite relieved in 1922, when another candidate was finally selected for the post. He explained that he had attended over 200 events that year, which included ninety-nine council meetings. During his tenure, his wife, Ada, whose maiden name Barnard was passed down through the generations, also

Bill Hobbs
Bill Hobbs (1863–1945) who, in his fifties, resigned as Mayor of Henley in order to fight in the First World War. (© Hobbs of Henley)

became a well-known local figure. In 1922, she was presented with a diamond and sapphire pendant in recognition for all her philanthropic work in the town.

Bill was made an Alderman in the mid-1920s and, after overcoming a serious but unspecified operation in 1927, he went on to serve until 1943, when he finally stood down, partly owing to his deafness. For many years he was also a borough and county magistrate, as well as a Justice of the Peace. When he finally passed away in 1945, Henley mourned the loss of one of the town's favourite sons. Furthermore, until being bedridden shortly before his death, he had continued to make a daily visit to the family business.[6]

Other

Bill, who lived for much of his life at 'The Gables' on St Andrews Road, had many other guises, including being a Freemason who served twice as the Worshipful Master of the Thames Lodge (as well as treasurer) and once as the Provincial Grand Wizard of Oxfordshire. He also was a member of the Ancient Order of Druids, the Royal Antediluvian Order of Buffaloes (with his brother Ernest), as well as being a Henley Charity Trustee and serving as chairman of the Old Henleiensians Association (for former Grammar School students).

The Wider Family

Bill was not the only one of his generation to be politically engaged, as a number of his brothers attended the Salisbury Club. Indeed, in the aftermath of the 1898 local election, Ernest was censured by magistrates for claiming the vote that came with Belmont House, despite making good money renting it out during the regatta. He went on to become a parish councillor at Shiplake (where Bill was briefly the local Conservative Association's treasurer) and was its ruling councillor in 1926. Furthermore, Arthur, who lived at the Cottage on Vicarage Road (sometimes listed as No. 22 St Mark's Road), served as the Head of the Ratepayer's Association in the Edwardian period. Around that time, the wives of Bill, Arthur, Ernest and Frederick were also active members of the Primrose League and the Henley Women's Unionist and Tariff Reform Association.

A. R. B. Hobbs (Dick)

Bill was entering the twilight of his political career in 1940, when his remaining son, Dick, who was already a member of the Ratepayer's Association, joined him on the town council, after being nominated to occupy a vacant seat. The *Henley and South Oxfordshire Standard* noted that as the latter was a local man, his personal interests were wrapped up in the town, while his age (forty) was also in his favour, given how elderly some of the others were. During the conflict, he also served as a Special Constable (with his cousin, Cyril), and as an officer in the Air Training Corps.

When it came to his subsequent re-election in 1945, Dick had a rather novel attitude to campaigning, as he told the local newspaper, 'I have not done any personal canvassing, as I feel the house-wife today has quite enough to do, with shopping and housework, without being disturbed by me knocking at your door asking for votes.' That did not stop him being elected and he went on to serve as mayor in 1952, 1953 and 1956 (the third son of a previous mayor to hold the top post). During his tenure, he organised the town's coronation festivities, which included hosting Princess Margaret when she planted the first of two turkey oak trees on Fair Mile (thereby replacing the elms), and running a water carnival that started at

Ald. A.R.B. Hobbs being presented to Her Majesty.

Queen Elizabeth Greeting Dick Hobbs, 1959
Councillor Dick Hobbs (1899–1969) being greeted by the Queen during her visit in 1959.
(© River and Rowing Museum, Henley-on-Thames)

Hobbs' yard. He was also a councillor when the Queen concluded her tour of Oxfordshire in the town in 1959. Dick also served as a magistrate for thirteen years (from 1954), Justice of the Peace for Oxfordshire, and chairman of the town's Primrose League.

He was known in the council for his 'keenness and enthusiasm', and when addressing Secondary Modern pupils in 1953, he shared that his personal motto was to be punctual, give your best and to be honest, bright and trustworthy. That was his recipe for being successful and making life worth living, while adding the practical advice of working hard in the day and using evenings for further education. He was also not afraid to embrace modern trends; in 1954, he was supportive of allowing event organisers to decide what dances were held in the Town Hall, after another councillor wanted to ban jiving on the premises.

Like his father, he personally knew many of the town councillors, as a number of them came from other well-known local families. In 1957, the mayor-elect, R. J. Pither, described how he and Dick had been banned from playing together as children, after they were caught 'strawberry scrumping'. Similarly, a decade later, when Dick was re-elected as mayor, councillor Green thanked him for the instruction he had received in the local Air Training Corps, which councillors Sadler and Lane had also benefitted from.

Dick, who spent much of his life at No. 35 Vicarage Road (near his cousin, Cyril, who resided at No. 28), also became Honorary Secretary of the Old Henleiensians Association (a post his nephew, Ron Drury, later held), as well as a governor at the Grammar School, chairman of the Henley Legion, Worshipful Master of the Thames Lodge of Freemasons, a member of the Ancient Order of Druids, and a representative of the Thames Conservancy for seven years from the early 1960s onwards. He was also the longest-serving councillor when he passed away suddenly in 1969, after a full day of work at the family business.[7]

The Wider Family

As in the previous generation, it was not simply one person who was politically active. Dick's wife, Edith, who was the daughter of councillor George Blackham, was also involved with civic affairs. As well as helping to entertain Princess Margaret during her visit, she became the Honorary Secretary of the Primrose League and the president of the women's section of the Henley branch of the British Legion. She was also a member of Holy Trinity Church, the Remenham Singers, and Cockpole Green's Women's Institute.

Although Dick's death ended the political involvement of those from the boat business, it was certainly not the final chapter of the family's public service. On the contrary, the following year, his daughter, Margaret Day, continued the tradition by joining Henley Borough Council (as a Conservative), which she said felt like the 'natural thing to do'. She came from a background in teaching and had previously been managing Holy Trinity School, having run a young mothers' group at Holy Trinity Church before that.

Her achievements included helping to start the Henley May Fair and fighting for the mayoralty to be retained, when the borough council was downgraded to a town council in 1974. Indeed, she was elected to the top post that year, which the *Henley Standard* described as a 'hat-trick for Hobbs'. She was a well-recognised figure in the town and became known as 'Mrs Tidy' (or the 'Litter Queen') for her tireless work in trying to keep Henley clean. Despite her many achievements, she modestly claimed that she was not particularly clever, serious, dynamic or even a passionate reformer, but that she was someone who enjoyed serving the town, who had common sense and competency. A room in Henley Town Hall was named after her and she was also a county councillor for many years.

In 1975, she was joined on the town council by her cousin, David Walden, whose career shared a number of similarities. He was also a Conservative, a county councillor, and Mayor of Henley – in his case twice (in 1980 and 1988). He was the son of Len Walden CBE, who was not only Dick's best man and husband of Marguerita Hobbs, but also president of the National Federation of Building Trades Employers. Like his father, David was involved with the same industry and was chairman of the National Accident Prevention Committee, president of the Reading branch of the National Federation of Building Trades Employers, and president of the local Rotary Club.[8]

W. A. B. Hobbs (Tony)

Dick was succeeded at the business by his son, Tony, who began working with him in Shiplake during the Second World War for a wage of one shilling a day (a lot of money for an eight-year-old boy). The latter went on to complete a five-year apprenticeship at the firm, which focused mainly on boatbuilding, but included some engineering. He then joined the Royal Marines as part of his National Service and fittingly spent much of his time on small boats on the Rhine, as an LCM (landing craft mechanised) coxswain. He then returned to the family firm to start the hire cruiser business, after his father had taken over the company.

Although he came from a long line of local politicians, he did not join the town council, but was instead involved in the civic affairs of the town in other ways. He was a trustee of the Henley Municipal Charities for over four decades (being its chairman for fifteen years) and he also became president of the Sea Cadets. He helped to form the local RNLI fundraising committee in 1975 (becoming its chairman) and, in 2004, his services to the town were recognised when he was honoured with a Henley town medal and an MBE. In 2012, he was featured in the *Faces of Henley* book that showcased a number of prominent local individuals.

In addition to his involvement in the sporting life of the town (see chapter 2), he was also made a Waterman to the Queen in 1981, which required him to attend many state functions, including transporting the monarch when she opened the Henley Royal Regatta headquarters in 1986 – when his portrait was painted by local artist Bill Mundy – and the Henley River and Rowing Museum in 1998. He also attended a function from Greenwich to Westminster Pier with Margaret Thatcher and the Queen of the Netherlands on board, as well as the VJ Day anniversary celebrations in 1990 that featured a fly-by by Concorde and Spitfires.

He continued as managing director until 1998, when Peter Herbert, the first non-family member to hold the post, took over. That was not the end of his active involvement with the firm, however, as he later joked that his subsequent retirement simply meant not having to work weekends.

J. R. B. Hobbs (Jonathan)

In 2012, the day-to-day running of the business passed down to Tony's son, Jonathan, the current managing director, who had joined the firm from university in 1993. He was involved with a whole variety of business ventures and was on the board of a number of limited companies connected with the firm, including Shiplake Court (from 2004), Rivertime Boat Trust (from 2005), Millpool Properties (2006–present) and Henley Boat Company (from 2013), as well as other wider initiatives associated with the town, such as the Henley Partnership, which turned into the Henley Business Partnership (from 2005–13), and the Spirit of Henley (from 2016). As that suggests, his tenure was marked by forging close ties with others in order to run a number of local events, such as in 2006, when he and commercial caterer Simon Cromack organised the first Henley Food Festival, which ran for a number of years. By 2015, he was also chairman of the

Tony Hobbs, 1986
A portrait of Tony Hobbs (b. 1932) in his Royal Waterman attire by William Mundy, in 1986.
(© River and Rowing Museum, Henley-on-Thames)

Jonathan and Suzy Hobbs
Jonathan and Suzy Hobbs enjoying some Mr Hobbs gin. (© Hobbs of Henley)

Passenger Boat Association and Visit Thames, as well as being the director of the Henley Music and Arts Festival and vice chairman of British Marine (Thames Valley). He was also a governor of Shiplake College (2007–18) and is currently one for the Oratory School (from 2018). Like his father, he too was made a Royal Waterman (in 2018).

Succession

As was the case with many Victorian businesses, the boat firm passed down the male line. One important reason for the longevity of Hobbs is that, unlike a number of its competitors, there were enough heirs to carry on the work. In fact, there were arguably too many in the early years, which not only forced a number of Harry's sons (and their children) into other careers, but also later led to some disputes about the ownership of the business. Initially, there may not have been much scope for assisting at the Ship, which may explain why Harry's first son, of the same name (b. 1861), became an ironmonger. By contrast, his fourth son, Frank (b. 1872), may have opted to become a tailor, as when he came of age there were already three family members at the relatively small boat business.

In 1901, when the firm was incorporated, it was jointly owned by Bill, Arthur and Harry, but the former is believed to have built up a controlling stake over the course of the early twentieth century. By 1918, his seniority was recognised in his wage of £400 compared to that of £350 for Arthur, while their younger brothers Ernest, Frederick and Albert also worked at the business. By 1931, Bill was in charge of the company's correspondence and account, as well as the buying of timber and the general superintendence of boatbuilding and woodwork repairs. Arthur, by contrast, dealt with the engineering works and any non-woodworking renovations and repairs. Under their direction was the youngest brother, Albert, who was given some oversight of repairs, and two of Arthur's sons, Cyril and John, who were used for 'various matters'. Further afield, Ernest was responsible for the 'efficiency and expansion' of the business at Shiplake, while Frederick was in charge of the same at Goring, in addition to the wet and dry docks at Springfield. An indication of the burgeoning number of family members at the firm, as well as how hard they had previously worked, was the decision in 1931 to allow directors to take an annual holiday.

With five brothers at the firm, many of their offspring unsurprisingly opted for other careers. Bill's oldest son, Reginald, became an accountant (a role he got through Hobbs' auditors), Arthur's sons briefly worked for the business before finding jobs in other Thames firms (as did their father), and Albert's son, Eddie, became a bank manager and acted as company chairman after the war. Indeed, the sheer number of family members involved with the firm in the 1930s eventually led to a dispute over control of the firm (see chapter 4), which resulted in Arthur resigning from the board early in 1945. Things could have turned out very differently, as Bill passed away only six months later. The loss of the senior figure at the firm created a considerable vacuum, not least because he personally handled much of the running of the business.

While Bill's shares were held in trust, Frederick, Dick and Albert were appointed as joint managing directors, although the former would pass away in 1948 and the latter five years later. In 1951, Dick consolidated his control of the firm by buying shares from the trustees of the late Arthur (used to cover the death duties), who had passed away the previous year. Furthermore, his wife, Edith, also came on board after the sale of her shop on the Reading Road enabled her to purchase Cyril's shares. Another family member who became a director in 1947 was Ron Drury, the son of Cassie Hobbs, who, after leaving the navy, was taken on by Bill. He was a very reliable man, who served as company secretary for many years; his daughter, Pamela, also worked in the office until they both retired in 1988.

Buying out the wider family may have been desirable for controlling the business and maintaining familial harmony, but it also reduced the number of potential heirs. There was no expectation that Dick's son, Tony, or grandson, Jonathan (the first to attend university), would join the business and, indeed, both considered other careers. After Dick died in 1969, Hobbs went through a difficult period, as there was only Tony (managing director) and Ron Drury (company secretary and director) running the business. Furthermore, the properties had become dilapidated and many boats required extensive refurbishment. Jackie Hobbs, Tony's wife, had small children to look after, but worked from home carrying out secretarial work. In 1974, Peter Herbert came to the business to help Tony and, soon after, Pamela Drury joined her father to run the administration and secretarial duties. After Ron and Pamela Drury both retired in 1988, Jackie Hobbs served as company secretary for a couple of years, before the firm's former bank manager, David Burnside, came to the business to assist with the accounts, along with his wife, Carol. They were succeeded by Steve Lock in 2012.

When Peter Herbert became managing director in 1998, Tony Hobbs explained that the firm was moving with the times by breaking with tradition. He was not the first non-family member to hold a senior post in the enterprise, as in the early twentieth century (1902–06), Frederick Hunter had been the company chairman.

The family retained the ownership of the business though, and, by 1974, Tony held 85.1 per cent of the ordinary shares. The only others with a stake were Eddie (6.6 per cent) and Ron Drury (8.3 per cent), as well a larger number of extended kin who had small numbers of preference shares that did not come with voting rights. By 2015 (after the demerger), Tony held 42.6 per cent of the shares in Hobbs of Henley, Jonathan and Jackie each had 25 per cent, while Pamela Drury owned 4.1 per cent and Wendy Pytches 3.3 per cent.[9]

Final Thoughts

In June 2013, the family gathered on board *Enchantress* and *New Orleans* for a trip to Temple Island to celebrate the eightieth birthday of Tony, the birthday of his daughter Melanie and the silver wedding anniversary of his other daughter, Katie. The event, which was naturally reported in the local press, brought together a dynasty that in the space of only two generations had gone from relative obscurity to becoming one of Henley's most distinguished families. Their tradition of public service, which stretched for almost a century, was started by Bill, a publican's son who became a notable pillar of the establishment. Indeed, it is their civic and charitable contributions to Henley life, rather than their business achievements, that are still one of the main sources of pride within the family today. Yet their own social standing was also bound up with the fortunes of their firm and it is to the contribution of those working in the 'Hobbs navy' that we turn in chapter 7.

Chapter 7

Workforce

…one of the main reasons for the longevity and success of Hobbs over the last 145 years has been that it has had vastly experienced watermen with real working knowledge of the Thames.

Jonathan Hobbs, 2015[1]

It is impossible to adequately sum up the collective recollections and experiences of hundreds of Hobbs employees spanning many decades, but you can give something of a flavour of

Workforce, 1936
The workforce in 1936, from left to right: Henry Hooper (sitting), Bert Hobbs (with hat), Charlie Pike, Lou Lightfoot (bottom), Bill Hinton, Bill Hobbs (in doorway), Dick Hobbs and Tom George (sitting). (© Hobbs of Henley)

Workforce, *c.* 1951
The workforce *c.* 1951. From left to right: Dick Manley, Ted Wise (sitting), Dick Hobbs, Chum Harvey (arms folded), Tony Porter (bottom), Bert Hobbs (in doorway), Tony Hobbs, Charlie Pike, Ron Drury (top, by window), Bill Hinton, Jim Piggott (sitting) and Les Smith. (© Hobbs of Henley)

what it was like being in this unusual working environment. Unfortunately, there are no early employment records to show the composition of the workforce, although Tony Hobbs recalls that the firm had around twenty-five staff members when Dick died (in 1969). That figure is close to the current (2019) number, although it swells to around fifty during the regatta week and falls back down to around ten in the winter.

Recruitment

A major challenge for any seasonal business like Hobbs is attracting good staff members, when year-round employment cannot necessarily be offered or guaranteed. As a result, the workforce was dominated by a more transient group of largely young men, who tended to stay for a number of seasons before moving on to other occupations. Summer jobs were particularly desirable for students or those who had other professions to fall back on. The latter included John Fenn, the Foreman of the piling gang, who used to joke that he 'always worked with water', as he reverted to being a plumber in the colder months. In recent years, some employees have been happy to alternate between spending the summer in Henley and the (British) winter in Australia.

In terms of recruitment, some staff members were trained in-house through official apprenticeships, like William Hooper, who was at Shiplake in 1924, and Colin Hinton, who started his (in marine engineering) in 1965, at the age of fifteen. Ray Gardiner started a six-year apprenticeship in the late 1950s, although his route to the firm was more unusual. He had been referred to the company by the labour exchange, but his case was helped by the fact that he was a gifted young footballer. When he visited the business, Dick Hobbs, the Mayor of Henley, recognised him, as he had presented him with a medal earlier that day for playing in a youth cup final.

The firm also attracted some staff members from other Thames businesses. One of the earliest employees was Charles Turner, a well-known boatbuilder who died in 1936, having worked his way around Shepherd and Dee, Hobbs, Arlett and Bushnell; he also constructed a model punt that was displayed in the Town Hall. Similarly, Harry Chapman, who died in 1933, had started at Searle's before moving to Hobbs' yard in Goring. When the company re-entered the passenger boat market at the end of the twentieth century, some employees inevitably came from other firms already specialising in that area, such as Peter West, the skipper of *Hibernia*, who cut his navigational teeth at Salters.

Others already had an interest in boats from elsewhere. One long-standing employee, Charles Pike (b. 1910), who built *Bosporos* and many cabin cruisers, learned his trade with the boat designer and sailing enthusiast Uffa Fox on the Isle of Wight, while Ray Cotton

Workforce, *c.* 1983
The workforce *c.* 1983. Sitting from left to right: Jeremy Fenn, Ray Cotton, Brian Denton, Ray Gardiner, Albert Cook and Kim Clifford; standing from left to right: Len Cripps, Derek Trimmings, Paul Baran, John Fenn, Colin Hinton, George Littleton, Ron Drury, Pamela Drury, Tony Hobbs, Andrew Trust and Peter Herbert. (© Hobbs of Henley)

Workforce, *c.* 1993
The workforce *c.* 1993. Front row from left to right: Len Cripps, Gill Charter, Keith Vaughan, Mark Halson, Colin Hinton, Harry Ridge and Kim Clifford; middle row from left to right: David Burnside, Ray Gardiner, Jackie Hobbs and Michael Lewington; back row from left to right: Peter Herbert, Jonathan Hobbs, Tony Hobbs, Darren Martin, Andrew Trust and John Trust. (© Hobbs of Henley)

came from J. S. White, another firm on the island. By contrast, Peter West was a keen rower who did a marine engineering apprenticeship at Salters and then worked as an Environment Agency tug driver, before moving to Hobbs. Another staff member who came with relevant training was Peter Herbert, who joined the firm in 1974, having graduated from the University of Southampton with a degree in Yacht and Boatyard Management.

Some employees came to Hobbs through their own family connections. Len Clark, who worked on the construction of the Regatta course from 1924, continued in the trade of his father, George, who retired in 1939 and, similarly, Colin Hinton joined the business because his father worked for Hobbs. Chummy Harvey, who began at the firm in the 1940s, followed in the footsteps of both his grandfather and father, as the former had been a Henley boat-letter and the latter had worked for the Thames Conservancy. In the modern era, it was not just male family members who worked for the firm: Kim Clifford, who joined Hobbs after doing work experience as a fifteen-year-old in the mid-1960s, was later joined by wife, Lisa, who became a passenger vessel coordinator. Furthermore, three of their sons also assisted with renting out craft.

The company looked to promote from within its ranks. Colin Hinton became the outboard services manager, for example, while Peter Herbert went from hiring out vessels on the waterfront in 1974 to eventually becoming managing director at the end of the twentieth century. Similarly, Kim Clifford became general manager in 2015, having worked in various roles, including skippering *Consuta II* and *New Orleans*.

Working Environment

The decline of many river-based trades meant that as the twentieth century progressed there were fewer competitors to which Hobbs might lose staff members. Although there was no large high-paying industry dominating the local economic scene, there were some prominent businesses that could attract workers with transferable skills, such as Stuart Turner, the engine manufacturer, and Walden, the builder. Nevertheless, staff retention was generally good and it was testament to the firm that the direction of traffic was often towards Hobbs, rather than away from it. Nevertheless, the company could only offer a small number of year-round jobs, which meant that only a few employees could make a career at Hobbs.

The staff members had to commit to a six-day week, which included weekends (when the pay was higher). The working hours, which were normally 8.30 a.m. to 5.30 p.m. (or a 7.30 a.m. start for the piling gang), actually increased for some of them at the end of the twentieth century, as the reintroduction of passenger boat services resulted in evening bookings.

The firm could not afford to pay high wages, although the skippers were on a better wage than some others on the river, such as their counterparts at Salters and the Environment Agency tug drivers. Furthermore, Hobbs tried to look after its workforce in other ways, such as providing senior staff members with private health care. There were also a number of perks for all employees, such as being able to use the rental craft for free and the passenger boats at a heavily discounted rate. Many of the workers confirmed that they were treated well. As Colin Hinton put it, 'The Hobbs family have been very good to me… I've been loyal to them and they have been loyal to me.' Indeed, Ray Gardiner recalled that when he was offered a job running a chandlery elsewhere, it was his respect for Tony Hobbs that led him to agree to do the job for the Henley firm instead.

The wages may have been low and the hours long, but these were not major problems, because the employees benefitted from being in a highly appealing working environment. Many of them were drawn by the prospect of being outside in the summer, while workers tended to be compensated for bad weather by being less busy.

The staff members were close-knit and felt like they were part of a family. They would often socialise together and occasionally the firm went on special outings. In July 1900, they enjoyed a day-trip to Folkestone organised by the Pleasant Sunday Afternoon Society, and in 1970 and 1995, some employees travelled to Guernsey to celebrate Hobbs' centenary and 125th anniversary respectively.

Being an umpire launch driver was an aspiration for many workers, as it was a prestigious role that required a high level of skill and carried a lot of responsibility. The honour was a particular highlight for those who experienced it, as you got to soak up the atmosphere from the 'best seat in the house' and you were often transporting important individuals. As a teenager, Tony Hobbs experienced the excitement for himself at the 1948 Olympics, as he was assigned to driving the judges back and forth. Chummy Harvey, a painter and varnisher who was in charge of *Magician* between 1950 and 1996, particularly enjoyed the adrenalin rush he felt as he went down the course to line up for the first race. He also described feeling 'ten feet tall' one year, when all the spectators' eyes were trained on his boat, as he transported Prince Rainier and Princess Grace of Monaco. It was not all plain sailing, however, as he was severely reprimanded once, after returning from lunch late, which required the other launches to be juggled. He saw himself as a faithful servant of the town, who loved the regatta and had enjoyed 'wonderful times with wonderful people over the years'. Another long-serving umpire launch driver was Colin Hinton, who became the lead driver and transported, among others, the Duke of Edinburgh, the Princess Royal, Prince Andrew, Sir Edward Heath, Dame Kelly Holmes, Sir Chris Hoy and Ruby Wax. He served Hobbs for over fifty years and like his bosses, Tony and Jonathan, was made a Royal Waterman (in 1996).

Although they were also on the water, those in the piling gang had a very different type of experience, as their job was very labour intensive. Their primary focus each year was preparing and dismantling the regatta course (from April to August), before doing additional jobs wherever they were needed. Len Clark recalled that one of his first tasks (in 1924) was straightening the course, at a time when they towed their workboat by hand. They would often sleep rough while out on the job, and were liable to be temporarily struck off if there was no work available out of season. Among those in the gang in the mid-twentieth century were Len Cripps and Harry Ridge, as well as John Fenn, who started as a temporary worker in 1956. When Fenn, who was a well-known angler and later president of the Henley Rotary Club (2010), became foreman, the pressure of the job initially caused him to direct the piling in his sleep! By 1984, the course required 540 wooden piles, 200 booms, 200 bolts, 400 hundredweight of nails, 200 buoys and 2 miles of wire cable. Indeed, when the Duke of Edinburgh asked him how he kept the piles so straight, he joked that he had a long piece of string! The two main challenges were the weather, as if it was raining it was not as easy to see if the piles were all lined up, and traffic on the Thames, as fast boats passing by made it more difficult to get the piles into position. He claimed the river could be like the M4 sometimes and despite gesticulating at some craft to slow down, many assumed he was being friendly and simply waved back. The task was even harder if the river was in flood; in 1985, two heavy pontoons that were waiting to be positioned broke away from their mooring in fast-flowing water. Fortunately, two locals prevented them from damaging a number of craft by fending them off until help arrived.

By the time the firm stopped the piling business (1988), it was already building up its passenger boat fleet, which opened up a new type of working environment. As in the navy, many of the crew members felt an attachment to their particular craft, each of which did different types of trip. The employees on board got to see more of the river, and working on private parties could be particularly enjoyable, especially during regattas and festivals, when they were able to experience the carnival atmosphere and sometimes receive tips. Kim Clifford recalled that one of his highlights was sailing past the Queen, when she visited the Henley Business School, as part of her diamond jubilee celebrations in 2012.

Naturally, the work environment was more conventional for engineers, like Cyril Twigg, who was at Hobbs in 1924. When the firm was still building boats, skilled workers were required, like Ernie Smith, a former Walden employee, who not only constructed cabinets and folding joints for craft, but also some high-end pieces of furniture. Even if they were not employed out on the waterfront, Ray Gardiner, who worked in the chandlery, stressed that all the employees were able to enjoy being *by* the Thames. In the summer, he often went swimming after work with other staff members, while the Henley Royal Regatta was always a particular highlight. At the showpiece event they were able to revel in the atmosphere that engulfed the whole town, while they were also able to join in with some of the festivities. They also sometimes participated in their own fun activities during the event, like holding running races up and down the rafted-up punts.

Even at quieter times, there was always something happening on the Thames, and it was this variety that appealed to many of the staff members. Peter Herbert described the job as being 'marvellously interesting', as you could be emptying a toilet one day and driving a film star the next. There was never a dull moment and, for many, being at Hobbs was more a way of life than an occupation. Peter Herbert summed up his experience as being a great deal of fun with too many highlights to mention.

Workforce, 2019
The workforce, 2019. Front row from left to right: Jackie Hobbs, Darren Martin, Michelle Patrick and Colin Hinton; middle row from left to right: Kim Clifford, Lisa Clifford, Peter Herbert and Tony Hobbs; back row from left to right: James Maudlin, Jonnie Oates, Peter West, Suzy Hobbs and Jonathan Hobbs. (© Hobbs of Henley)

Occupational Hazards

The work environment may have been extremely enjoyable, but it was not without its dangers. Drownings were a regular occurrence on the Thames, which is why Henley started a river rescue service in 1976. By virtue of being on the waterfront, the employees of Hobbs were occasionally confronted by distressing circumstances. In 1886, for example, Arthur Hobbs spotted the body of a fourteen-year-old boy in the river and helped to retrieve it. Indeed, when people disappeared on the waterway, the firm often assisted with the search. In 1892, for example, Arthur helped to drag the Thames for a corpse, after he was unable to get to a swimmer in time, who he had seen get into trouble from afar. The man, George Wright, had just been released from the Reading gaol and had initially seemed fine, having jumped in off the bridge. Similarly, in 1940, a woman drowned after attempts to resuscitate her were unsuccessful, despite Arthur and a Mr Hooper reaching her quickly.

Accidents occasionally happened to clients too. In 1902 and 1924 similar deaths occurred after a customer fell out of a rented canoe. Fatalities were not always the result of drowning, however, as in 2017, the publican of the Old Bell, Rob Myles-Hooton, collapsed and died from a brain haemorrhage while on his boat *Lola Belle*, which was moored up at the Hobbs yard. There were no river-related deaths among staff members, but, in 1975, the firm lost a twenty-one-year-old employee, Guy Rowell, in a car crash only three weeks into his job.

There were also many close shaves on the river, such as in 1961, when one of the firm's punts was struck and capsized by *Mapledurham*, a large Salters passenger boat. A seventeen-month-old baby was fortunate to remain floating on a cushion – like Moses in the Bible, as one newspaper suggested. Another collision occurred at the Henley Regatta in 1978, the same year two female rowers almost succeeded in being admitted to the male-only event. A customer who rented a motorboat from Hobbs lost control of it and entered the part of the course that was not protected by booms. The final of the Thames Cup was underway and the craft was struck by Leander, which broke an oar, and forced the race to be re-run.

Although there were numerous drownings and near misses, the firm also helped to avert a number of catastrophes. One of the earliest recorded rescues was in May 1886, when a young girl fell into the water after playing on Lion Meadow. Workmen alerted Arthur Hobbs, who was working by Webb's Wharf on the opposite side of the river, and he quickly got to the exhausted child before it was too late. A similar incident occurred in 1907, this time to the four-year-old son of Sidney Holton, the grocer on Friday Street. No adult was around, but Albert Hobbs and Henry Hooper saw the child struggling and the former got to him by plunging into the river, just as he sank into deep water.

Ernest Hobbs was involved in one of the most unusual rescues involving a horse and cart, in June 1904. The driver was Mr Barefield, an employee of Mr Walden (the builder) whose son, Len, would unite two major Henley firms by marrying Bill Hobbs' daughter, Marguerita. The horse had been taken into the river but drowned after somehow getting off its feet and into deep water. As the cart began to sink Barefield, in desperation, was forced to throw his young child into the water, where Ernest collected him. The latter was involved with another successful rescue three years later in Shiplake, when a charwoman got into trouble after accidentally falling into the water from the top of a houseboat.

Sometimes the firm came to the aid of distressed individuals who were in danger but had managed to find something to temporarily hold onto until help arrived. In June 1893, one of the Hobbs brothers went to the assistance of double scullers who had capsized after catching a crab, with the non-swimmer clinging onto his crew mate. Similarly, in 1908, Arthur Hobbs and Alfred Parrott responded to the screams of a lady who had fallen in, but had managed to hold onto the side of a launch. In December 1931, the former and his three sons performed a daring rescue in Marlow after a racing eight from Marlow Rowing Club was swept against the weir, known as the 'lion's mouth'. The operation, which took over an hour, was watched by many onlookers from the bridge.

A rather more amusing and novel rescue of an oarsman occurred in 1933, when an employee, T. George, went to the assistance of Dennis Guye, the British amateur sculling champion, who had invoked the wrath of a passing swan. The famous sportsman had inadvertently rowed towards some cygnets, which provoked the cob to wreak his revenge by knocking him into the river and proceeding to peck him in a frenzied and prolonged attack. The Wingfield scull champion was forced to repeatedly duck under the hull of his boat, until help from Hobbs arrived.

The firm also assisted in a number of instances when boats got wedged across Henley Bridge in fast-flowing water. The help was not always successful, however, as sometimes the Hobbs craft were not powerful enough, such as when the Salters passenger boat *Henley* got stuck in 1979. By 2007, the firm had more substantial boats and the crew of *New Orleans* (Kim Clifford and Simon Dudding) were praised for getting a line to and towing to safety the cabin cruiser *Ahminah* after it capsized near Marsh Lock with six people on board. The following year, within the space of a week, Kim and Darren Martin went to the assistance of four pensioners in trouble on a hire boat, and two rowers who fell into the water after their double sculling boat had capsized.

A further two traumatic incidents occurred from the towpath in 2017. In October, a seventy-two-year-old man suffering from Parkinson's became submerged in the water with his wheelchair on top of him, after the wheel caught in a crack. Various members of the public went to his assistance, including Ben Wiltshire, a Hobbs skipper, who helped retrieve the wheelchair. Further drama occurred six weeks later when a pram rolled into the Thames by Mill Meadows, at a time when few people were around. The mother managed to unstrap the baby and get him to safety, but was unable to pull herself out over the high riverbank. Her cries were heard on the other side of the river by Andy Trust, the boatyard services manager at Hobbs, who contacted the office on Station Road. Jonathan Hobbs and Kim Clifford ran to assist, while Trust and Darren Martin crossed the river on a powered dinghy.[2]

Final Thoughts

Over the years, many individuals have been connected with Hobbs, as the firm has provided an important source of employment in the local area. In 2016, a joint event at the Leander Club was held to celebrate the long service of Peter Herbert and Colin Hinton whose working knowledge of the river had been invaluable to the business. Yet the respect and appreciation went both ways, as they were among the many staff members who spoke in glowing terms about their experiences at the firm.

As has been shown, the workforce also played its part in trying to keep people safe on the waterway. Despite not receiving any recognition from the Royal Humane Society, it is clear that the quick thinking and prompt action of many individuals saved the lives of a number of people.

Conclusion

No matter where one went on the river, everybody knew Mr Hobbs' firm...
Henley and South Oxfordshire Standard, 1945[1]

Historic firms tend to exude an air of timelessness, continuity and permanence, but few survive without considerable diversification and hard graft. Even though the Hobbs family had the river 'in their blood', that was no guarantee of long-term success. Indeed, one estimate in 1996 suggested that only around one in seven family firms reaches a third generation and, as has been shown, many prominent and well-known river businesses in Henley did not stand the test of time.

In 2017, Jonathan Hobbs was asked why he thought his firm had survived as long as it had. While acknowledging the crucial role the workforce played, he stressed the importance of knowing your market, doing your research, studying and learning from competitors, and striving to be the best in your field. He added that you also needed to be astute, brave and sensible. These traits neatly capture the ethos of a business that took risks to expand and develop, but without becoming overstretched or allowing its ambitions to extend too far beyond the horizons of its original market, the one it knew best.

Hobbs was founded on the two core industries of Henley (beer and boats) and its early growth was closely connected with the transformation of the town into a highly fashionable riverside resort. The firm benefitted from the vast numbers of visitors who flocked to the waterway during the so-called 'golden age of the Thames'. Under the management of the remarkable Bill Hobbs, the business established a position of dominance by the introduction of new services and astute property investments. The expansion to sites outside of Henley led the firm to become, for a time, one of the largest providers of pleasure boat accommodation on the Thames with sizeable rental fleets in a number of locations. The second half of the twentieth century was more challenging, as although Hobbs was never in financial peril, there were only just enough heirs to keep the business going. Most of the property empire was sold and while some activities were stopped, like boatbuilding, others were started, like cabin cruiser rental. The firm's fortunes were boosted by the river's popularity in the 1970s and a new chapter in Hobbs' history opened in 1980, when passenger boat services were reintroduced and then subsequently expanded. Although the company had already eclipsed most of the local competition by that point, the development enabled Hobbs to drive home its advantage by carrying far greater numbers of customers, offering a greater range of revenue-producing options, and embracing new marketing opportunities. The desire to innovate also helped the company avoid the kind of conservatism that can so often blight long-standing family firms. The attitude was summed up by Tony Hobbs, who in 1998 told a reporter that he believed that if you stood still in business, you got left behind.

A poignant demonstration of how much the firm had changed was given in 2007, when Jonathan Hobbs described it as a 'hospitality company'. This important repositioning in the market led the business to focus on offering clients a range of river experiences that appealed to people's imaginations in what was already a highly evocative location. In that sense, the firm benefitted greatly from the overall mystique surrounding Henley (as a regatta town), which a 1996 survey showed was what many local businesses believed was *the* main advantage of being based there. The rebranding of the boat company as 'Hobbs of Henley' emphasised that close connection, which the family's long-standing commitment to local civic affairs had already helped to cement. Yet the business also played its own important part in shaping the same idealised perception of the town that it benefited from. It did this not only by influencing the appearance of the famous waterfront, but in offering new 'high-end' services that appealed to and reinforced the stereotype, while significantly enhancing its own reputation. These included an upmarket restaurant (on its premises), luxurious private charters, an exclusive rental experience in the form of the Henley Boat Club, and the town's first premium gin.

The latter represented a new milestone in leveraging and promoting the firm's own history, as a way of establishing that the company has been a key part of the same Thames tradition that forged the town's reputation. That continuity between past and present was further emphasised in some of the digital marketing that stressed that the company had moved with the times, but was still 'steeped in history' and had not lost the standards of service set by its 'forefathers from the Victorian and Edwardian eras'.

In that respect, this book is a further testament to the considerable contribution made by a Thames dynasty dating back almost 400 years that is deeply woven into the very fabric of Henley. While their contribution to opening up the waterway to hundreds of thousands of visitors may be obvious, as has been shown, there are many other areas of local life where those connected with the firm have left their mark, including saving lives. If you are involved with local charitable causes, participate in key events in the social calendar like the Royal Regatta, May Fair or half marathon, visit the River and Rowing Museum, attend one of the town's football, rugby or rowing contests, enjoy the Henley music or arts scene, use council facilities like Mill Meadows or the Town Hall, or simply appreciate the beauty of the famous riverside vista, you can be relatively confident that a member of the Hobbs family has had something to do with it. Indeed, it is entirely appropriate to celebrate the legacy of a business that has become synonymous with the regatta town, and also one of the most notable families associated with the royal River Thames.[2]

Endnotes

Introduction

1. Hickman and Kinch, *A Guide to Henley and its Vicinity* (Henley-on-Thames, 1838).
2. Citations in this study have been condensed down and the main works are listed in the Bibliography.
3. Information from Balliol College's archive and a history of Burrow Farm commissioned by David Palmer.
4. From parish and census records, *Posse Comitatus, Bucks Herald*, 7 June 1890, and *Reading Mercury*, 23 May 1840, 16 March 1845, 29 April 1871 and 27 September 1890.
5. *Henley-on-Thames: Official Guide* (Henley, 1936), p. 46 and *Oxfordshire Directory* 1958-9, p. 275.
6. S. Townley, *Henley-on-Thames: Town, Trade and River* (London, 2009), p. 141.

Chapter 1

1. www.thames.me.uk (accessed 28 August 2019).
2. C. Dickens, *Dickens' Dictionary of the Thames* (London, 1885).
3. Hickman and Kinch, *Guide to Henley* (1866) and E. Climenson, *A Guide to Henley-on-Thames* (Henley-on-Thames, 1896), pp. 78-80.
4. For more on the statistics, see S. Wenham, 'Oxford, the Thames and Leisure: a History of Salter Bros, 1858-2010' (Oxford University DPhil thesis, Michaelmas term 2012).
5. J. and E. R. Pennell, *The Stream of Pleasure* (London, 1891), p. 125.
6. G. D. Leslie, *Our River* (London, 1881), p. 123 and *The Pall Mall Gazette*, 1 October 1886. For more on the popularisation of camping on the river, see S. Wenham 'The River Thames and the Popularisation of Camping, 1860–1980', *Oxoniensia* LXXX (2015).
7. Quoted in *Henley Standard*, 4 August 1922.
8. N. Wigglesworth, *The Social History of Rowing* (London, 1992), p. 96, Townley, *Henley*, p. 145, *Henley Standard*, 13 March 1908, 17 December 1909, 10 July 1914 and 4 August 1922, and *Lock to Lock Times*, 4 July 1891.
9. www.wargravehistory.org.uk/B-17.html (accessed 28 August 2019), and *Henley Standard*, 15 November 1918 and 11 May 1945.
10. River and Rowing Museum Thames Conservancy General Report of the Conservators year ending December 1973, p. 4, J. H. B. Peel, *Portrait of the Thames* (London, 1967), p. 14, *Henley Standard*, 5 April 1973, 22 December 1979 and 27 June 2003, River Thames Alliance, *Thames Waterway Plan 2006-2011* (2005), p. 56 and Townley, *Henley*, p. 173.
11. *Henley Standard*, 13 August 1954.
12. *Financial Times*, 4 October 2013.
13. Hobbs Directors' Book and *Henley Standard*, 30 August 1985, 15 July 1994, 25 August 1995 and 25 July 1997.
14. Hobbs Directors' Book, 18 July 1973, *Henley Standard*, 10 July 1953, 27 April and 4 May 1973, 30 July 1976, 5 December 1980, 25 July 1997, 24 May 2009 and 21 May 2015, and *Thames Waterway Plan 2006-2011*.

Chapter 2

1. Climenson, *Guide to Henley*, p. 1.
2. Wigglesworth, *Social History of Rowing*, p. 66 and *Henley Standard*, 29 August 1913, 31 October 1952 and 16 April 1954.
3. *Henley Standard*, 9 and 23 April 1887, and 1 November 1907.
4. R. Burnell, *Henley Royal Regatta* (London, 1989), p. 8.
5. *The Boater*, March 2000 and *Daily Telegraph*, 28 June 1922.
6. *Henley Standard*, 4 June 2014 and *Henley Advertiser*, 25 June 1898, 12 August 1899, 13 September 1902 and 3 June 1905.
7. *Jackson's Oxford Journal*, 15 May 1824, *Henley Advertiser*, 24 August 1895 and 17 May 1902, *Henley Standard*, 3 July 2017, and *Rowing*, April 1971.
8. *Henley Standard*, 8 November 1929 and 12 August 2019.
9. Ibid., 31 July 1914 and 17 August 1934.
10. Ibid., 27 November 1896, 21 January and 14 May 1920, 23 July 1920 and 26 May 2014.
11. Ibid., 15 April 1898, 20 February 1904, 8 January 1908 and 20 February 1981.
12. Ibid., 20 February 1904, 8 January 1908 and 17 June 1910.

Chapter 3

1. Climenson, *Guide to Henley*, pp. 59-60.
2. *Kelly's Directory of Berkshire, Buckinghamshire and Oxfordshire* 1887, p. 641 and *Royal Thames Guide* (London, 1899), p. 137.
3. *Daily Telegraph*, 27 May 1904.
4. R. T. Rivington, *Punting* (Oxford, 1983), p. 34.
5. *Henley Standard*, 8 February 1924.
6. Many of the boats in this section are mentioned in the Thames Vintage Boat Club registers (of past and present members), *The Boater*, March 2000, and *Henley Standard*, 17 July 1987 and 23 June 1989.
7. *Henley Official Guide* (1967), p. 44 and interview with Ray Gardiner, 29 August 2019.
8. *Henley Standard*, 18 July 1952, 4 April 1980, 29 June 1990, 4 July 2008 and 10 May 2013. For more on the umpire launches see www.consuta.org.uk/Archives/The%20Henley%20Umpire%20launches.PDF and www.wargravehistory.org.uk/jan17.html (accessed 30 August 2019).
9. *Henley Standard*, 28 June 1895, 14 June 1907, 19 February 1971, 19 August 1981, 5 February 1982, 12 March and 3 June 1982.

Chapter 4

1. Quoted in *Henley Standard*, 4 August 1922.
2. *Henley Standard*, 16 August 1884, 29 July and 19 August 1893, 19 October and 30 November 1894, 18 August 1899, 27 July 1906, 20 August 1909, 4 February 1910 and 12 May 1961.
3. *Henley Advertiser*, 25 June 1898, 12 August 1899, 13 September 1902 and 3 June 1905, and *Henley Standard*, 12 May 1961 and 4 June 2014.
4. *Henley Standard*, 28 May 1993.
5. *Henley Standard*, 23 November 1984 and *Henley Herald*, 3 April 2014.
6. *Henley Standard*, 29 July 1927, 14 June 1940, 4 April 1947, 11 March 1959, 20 February 1987, 7 August 1998 and 18 June 1999.
7. *Daily Telegraph*, 28 June 1922, *Daily Mail*, 17 June 2017, and *Henley Standard*, 28 May 1993, 24 August 2012 and 29 June 2015.

Chapter 5

1. Townley, *Henley*, p. 162.
2. *The Boater,* March 2000, Hobbs Directors' Book, *Henley Standard*, 15 July 1904, and *Daily Telegraph*, 27 May 1904.
3. *Henley Standard*, 1 September 2014.
4. Records from Companies House and *Henley Standard*, 26 March 1897, 6 April 1900 and October 1962.
5. *Henley Standard*, 15 July 1988, and Hobbs Directors' Book.
6. *Henley Standard*, 27 January 1906, 24 April 1953, 21 June 1956, 14 June 1985, 6 August 2004 and 4 December 2017.
7. *Henley Advertiser*, 16 October 1875, 14 April 1888, 24 May 1890, 28 March 1891, 26 September 1919 and 13 September 1935.
8. *Henley Standard*, 2 December 1966 and 21 February 1986.

Chapter 6

1. *Henley Standard*, 12 January 1979.
2. Ibid., 2 January 1897, 20 January 1905 and 22 April 1910.
3. Ibid., 12 February 1904 and 14 November 1913.
4. Ibid., 17 and 31 May 1907, 13 March 1908, 20 May 1910 and 11 February 1910.
5. *Reading Mercury*, 22 August 1914 and 9 November 1918, *Henley Standard*, 29 September 1900, 25 September 1914 and 27 July 1917, *Daily Telegraph*, 28 July 1915, *Kingston Daily Gleaner*, 15 March 1915 and G. K. Rose, *The Story of the 2/4th Oxfordshire and Buckinghamshire Light Infantry* (Oxford, 1920).
6. *Henley Standard*, 15 December 1922 and 31 August 1945.
7. Ibid., 31 October 1947, 17 July 1953, 15 January 1954, 24 May 1957, 10 April 1959 and 27 June 1969.
8. Ibid., 1 February 1957, 12 January 1979 and 9 May 1980.
9. Hobbs Directors' Book, interviews with the family, Companies House documents and *Henley Standard*, 7 August 1998.

Chapter 7

1. *Henley Standard*, 28 April 2015. This chapter draws from information from the *Henley Standard* and interviews given by employees throughout the years, as well as ones conducted by the author with Tony and Jonathan Hobbs, Peter Herbert, Peter West and Ray Gardiner.
2. *Reading Evening Post*, 11 April 1975, and *Henley Standard*, 3 July 1886, 16 June and 9 September 1893, 30 August 1902, 11 June 1904, 26 April 1907, 25 September 1908, 25 April 1924, 29 March 1943, 16 June 1961, 7 July 1978, 13 April 1979, 31 August 2007 and 23 January 2017.

Conclusion

1. *Henley Standard*, 31 August 1945.
2. Institute of Directors, *Family Businesses* (London, 1996), p. 5, and *Henley Standard*, 12 January 1996, 7 August 1998, 14 September 2007 and 23 October 2017.

Bibliography

Short 'potted histories' of Hobbs of Henley can be found in the *Thames Guardian* (spring 1998) and *The Boater* (March 2000). The references in this work have been condensed down, but full citations can be found at www.simonwenham.com. The main sources of this book were local newspapers, especially the *Henley Standard* (from 1956) and its predecessor the *Henley and South Oxfordshire Standard* (both referred to as *Henley Standard* in the endnotes), as well as the *Henley Advertiser* and the *Reading Mercury*. One of the best histories of the town is Simon Townley's *Henley-on-Thames: Town, Trade and River* (London, 2009), but other key resources include the following:

Andrew, M., *Henley-on-Thames* (Salisbury, 2005)

Blomfield, D., 'Tradesmen of the Thames: Success and Failure Among the Watermen and Lightermen Families of the Upper Tidal Thames 1750-1901' (Kingston University PhD thesis, 2006)

Bolland, R. R., *Victorians on the Thames* (Tunbridge Wells, 1994)

Burstall, P., *The Golden Age of the Thames* (London, 1981)

Climenson, E. J., *A Guide to Henley-on-Thames* (Henley, 1896)

Cottingham, A., *The Hostelries of Henley* (Shiplake, 2000)

Dix, F., *Royal River Highway* (Newton Abbot, 1985)

Dodd, C., *Henley Royal Regatta* (London, 1989)

Hazeldine, E., *Henley-on-Thames Through Time* (Stroud, 2014)

Heywood, A., *Abel Heywood's Guide to Henley-on-Thames* (London, 1882)

Hickman and Kinch, *A Guide to Henley upon Thames and Its Vicinity* (Henley, 1838 and subsequent dates)

Preston, M., *Three Men and a Boat* (Henley, 2017)

Salter, J., *A Guide to the River Thames* (London, 1884 and subsequent editions)

Thacker, F. S., *The Thames Highway*, volume I and II (London, 1914 and 1920)

Wenham, S., 'Oxford, the Thames and Leisure: A History of Salter Bros, 1858-2010' (Oxford University DPhil thesis, Michaelmas term 2012)

Wenham, S., *Pleasure Boating on the Thames: A History of Salter Bros, 1858-Present Day* (Stroud, 2014 and 2017)

Wenham, S., 'The River Thames and the Popularisation of Camping, 1860–1980' *Oxoniensia* LXXX (2015)

Wheeler, R. L., *From River to Sea: The Marine Heritage of Sam Saunders* (Newport, 1993)

Whitehead, D. C., *Henley-on-Thames: A History* (Chichester, 2007)

Wigglesworth, N., *The Social History of Rowing* (London, 1982)

Wilson, D. G., *The Thames: A Record of a Working Waterway* (London, 1987)

There are also many good online resources, including collections of newspapers (e.g. www.britishnewspaperarchive.co.uk and www.gale.com/intl/c/british-library-newspapers-part-i), as well as websites dedicated to the Thames (e.g. www.thames.me), umpire boats (e.g. www.consuta.org.uk) and the Henley area (e.g. www.british-history.ac.uk/vch/oxon/vol16, www.henleycensus.info and www.FriethHistory.org).

Acknowledgements

Firstly, I would like to thank Connor Stait, Louis Archard and the team at Amberley Publishing for producing the book, and the directors of the firm, Tony and Jonathan Hobbs, for permission to write the history and for providing access to the company archive. I am also very grateful to the many people who have given invaluable help: Clare and David Wenham for their editing and advice; Mark Smith, Chris Day, Richard Carwardine, Peter Southwell and Ian Farrell for encouraging my historical research; Mark Lawrence and the Oxfordshire History Centre team for the special arrangement for viewing the microfilms; the staff at the Bodleian Library and the Buckinghamshire and Berkshire Record Offices; past and present employees of Hobbs, including Peter Herbert, Ray Gardiner, Michelle Patrick, Peter West, and Kim and Lisa Clifford; the Thames Traditional Boat Association and Thames Vintage Boat Club; and those who have given permission to use images, including Katherine Robson of the River and Rowing Museum, Peter Delaney of Wargrave Local History Society, Lauren Dolman and Amy Boylan of Balliol College, Axel Fithen of the *Henley Standard*, Sue Milton of www.thames-cards.co.uk, Suzy Hobbs and Rupert Stevens. Lastly, and most importantly, I must thank my wife, Angela, and sons, Benjamin and Isaac, for the support, love and encouragement, and for putting up with the imposition of another historical study.

About the Author

Simon Wenham is on the part-time tutor panel of Oxford University's Continuing Education department, where he teaches courses on Victorian Britain. He worked on the Thames for a number of years as operations manager for Salters Steamers Ltd and has travelled on the river by skiff, steamer, motor boat, punt, canoe and narrowboat. Simon's doctoral research at the university was turned into the book *Pleasure Boating on the Thames: A History of Salter Bros 1858–Present Day* (2014) and he has also written a number of history articles, including an academic work on the popularisation of camping on the waterway. He has done research for a variety of authors and media companies, and he was also on the Scientific Committee of the 'European Rivers and Towns' initiative. Simon has been a regular contributor to Radio Oxford and has featured in a number of televised documentaries, including one for Channel 5 that involved talking to Tony Robinson about history while punting down the River Cherwell. As well as giving popular-level talks on a variety of historical subjects, he maintains www.simonwenham.com, which promotes aspects of social history with a particular emphasis on Victorian Britain, the River Thames, Oxford and the development of leisure. Simon lives in Oxford with his wife Angela and two children.